Charles Van Norden

The Outermost Rim and Beyond

A Contribution toward Patience, Reverence, Silence and Spirituality

Charles Van Norden

The Outermost Rim and Beyond
A Contribution toward Patience, Reverence, Silence and Spirituality

ISBN/EAN: 9783337425524

Printed in Europe, USA, Canada, Australia, Japan

Cover: Foto ©Lupo / pixelio.de

More available books at **www.hansebooks.com**

AND BEYOND.

A CONTRIBUTION TOWARD PATIENCE, REVERENCE, SILENCE AND SPIRITUALITY, IN THE STUDY OF NATURE AND OF GOD.

BY

CHARLES VAN NORDEN.

"Philosophy begins in wonder."—PLATO.

NEW YORK:
ANSON D. F. RANDOLPH & COMPANY,
900 BROADWAY, COR. 20th STREET.

PREFACE.

The following treatise is only a contribution toward reverential thought upon divine things and not an effort to end controversy. What it omits of sacred truth is not, therefore, to be held as denied, doubted or even slighted; and what it dwells upon is not purposely pushed forward into relatively undue prominence.

This little work does not presume to rebuild the ruins of the observatories of this or that school, but rather to show that patience and reverence and spirituality can study the heavens anywhere in the open fields. It is written in hope that it may strengthen faith and courage in the hearts of some that falter, panic-stricken over the perils which in this age beset the cause of religion; and it utters the firm and calm belief of the author, that, though stand-points may change and conceptions enlarge, the Truth will prevail.

St. Albans, Vt.

TABLE OF CONTENTS.

PART FIRST.
THE OUTERMOST RIM.

Chap. I.—The Horizon, ... 7
" II.—Widening Horizons, . . . 18
" III.—The Mystery of Nature, . . 29
" IV.—The World's Shadow, . . . 47

PART SECOND.
VOICES FROM BEYOND.

Chap. V.—Hints of God in Physical Nature, ... 55
" VI.—Hints of God in the Moral Nature of Man, . . . 68
" VII.—The Teachings of the Religious Nature, ... 87
" VIII.—God in History, ... 102

PART THIRD.

THE MYSTERY OF GODLINESS.

Chap. IX.—Inspired Genius,	121
" X.—The Unexpected Christ,	134
" XI.—Christ as an Epoch-Maker,	151
" XII.—The Truth in Parable,	163
" XIII.—The Authority of Christ,	182
" XIV.—The Mysteries of Christ,	189
CONCLUSION,	205

THE OUTERMOST RIM.

PART I.

CHAPTER I.

THE HORIZON.

" What an enigma then is man ! What a strange chaotic, and contradictory being ! Judge of all things, feeble earth-worm ! depository of truth, mass of uncertainty! glory and butt of the Universe ! If he boast himself, I abase him ; if he humble himself, I glory in him ; and I always contradict him till he comprehends that he is an incomprehensible monster."—PASCAL.

ON the eastern shore of the Lake of Geneva there stands well-preserved an ancient castle, with draw bridge and moat, with turrets and donjon-keep. Time has dealt gently with Chillon, and the storms of ages have but roughened its walls for creepers and lichens. It rises from the blue waters of Leman in the foreground and contrasts with the green slopes of Villeneuve in the background—colossal, formidable and picturesque as of old.

On one summer's day, three men of different

moods strolled through its precincts and pondered its memories. The first was a disciple of utility—a statistician, who had won for himself a name for unusual common sense. He entered the ancient archway with critical eye, measuring-tape in hand; and, as he paced the courts and climbed the rude stairways and looked down from the battlements, he soliloquized thus:

"These massive walls—how they tell of an age of despotic sway over brute strength! This desolate banquet-hall—what an unkempt herd of ruffians was wont to gather around the oaken board! And this ladies' boudoir, without carpet and without pictures—how comfortless and dreary! Poor little women! how they must have twirled and tugged at these old spinning-wheels to keep their untidy men-at-arms in clean homespun! How long could such a fortification as this have held out against a well-equipped force of French or Italian chivalry? So much beef and so much pork and so much grain would have been needed month by month. Water at least must have been plenty, drawn up from the profound depths under the western wall. Ah, here is the armory! These are the breast-plates, helmets, and greaves of mediæval war. Very small, all of them! They could not be worn by an average soldier in any American regiment of to-day. The famous knights of old were short and slight. The times have manifestly bettered. Doubtless this is owing to cleaner and warmer homes, wholesomer food, purer habits, improved pathology, and especially to the less frequent slaughter of the vigorous men. What a rude age it was—poor in resources, feeble in brain-power, and barbarous in spirit!"

And the man of common sense went forth content with the present, and with no shadow of regret over the past or any of its belongings.

The second traveller was a poet. He saw with his imagination and measured with his fancy. The ivy on the walls, the lichens and mosses that had overgrown clammy nooks and the crumbling battlements, all served to dismiss the present; and the past was come again. He bowed over the parapet and gazed down into the blue depths of the water beneath; he scanned pensively the chaplet of mountain peaks that crowned the glorious landscape; and lo, the little steamer down on the lake, that panted inward toward the landing-place laden with tourists, was become a barge, rowed by men in white, and bearing the lord of the land and his beautiful lady to the baronial hall. Overhead streamed again in the sunshine the ancient banner, embroidered with the ancestral coat-of-arms; and from the silent court below came up the old hum of many voices. Ere long, instead of a host of tourists, all agape with curiosity, and red guide-book in hand, the lord and his lady and many a goodly knight and dame and man-at-arms, seemed to march in gay procession over the drawbridge and through the archway into the castle court. And now the men were in the hall, whole sides of beef steaming on the oaken tables, and wine poured forth like water; with boisterous merriment and rude uncanny wit, they crammed their bodies with coarse food. And here above, in the quiet of the boudoir, the ladies assembled. Yonder against the wall was a little shrine in ivory, and Jesus crucified, and here a shrine in ebony of a saint. On this side and on that hung long, heavy arras—and yonder stood a Venetian mirror. A carved cabinet of exquisite workmanship, the product of endless labor, contained my lady's finery. Here they were sitting, by this ample window, to look out upon as lovely a view as ever greeted mortal eye, the lady and her maids, delicate tissues adorning her graceful person, a coronet of gold bestud with gems gracing her fair brow, and embroidery of exquisite pattern employing her white fingers. And now the lay of the minstrel was heard, and now the clash of the tournament, and again in the silent night the serenade. And the poet went forth, dreams of woman's beauty and of man's prowess, and of all the glitter and gayety of the ancient chivalry, rendering tame the present and glorifying the past; and he murmured:

> "Thrilling days, those days of old,
> For ladies fair and warriors bold."

The third traveller was a sad man, a person of active sympathies, a philanthropist. He neither measured nor idealized the old fortress: he thought mostly of the poor serfs out beyond, in the wretched huts, that time had mercifully swept away. He reflected, that the few revelled and the many toiled.

My lord and my lady pursued a careless life amid plenty and in idleness; but their prosperity was wrung with mailed hand and iron heel out of their despised vassals and their weaker neighbors. Every stone in the massive walls seemed to echo back the blow of a lash and a groan; every old piece of armor seemed covered with the blood-stains of murder and robbery. He went down into the accursed dungeon, and gazed with horror upon the pillars to which wretches had been chained in a living death, for no other cause than to gratify the vengeance or to serve the interests of my lord. He peered with blanched face into the noisome hole where the executioner did his horrid work, and looked out upon the calm lake through the opening in the cellar wall, whence the headless body was thrust forth. Here they died, condemned by their enemy, without judge or jury. "Let the stones crumble," he cried; "let the archways fall; let the walls be shaken of an earthquake and come down; let the keep be riven of lightnings, and let lichens and mosses and ivies hide out of sight this monument of ancient injustice! On the ruins of this colossal tyranny let there spring up a modern city, granting equal rights to all, in its civil liberties, its freedom of worship, and its general good-will and prosperity, affording a glorious contrast to the old-time barbarity that has been, and, thanks to God, is gone!"

And the philanthropist shook off the dust of his feet against the castle, and hurried out into the free sunshine.

And all three travellers judged wisely, each from his own stand-point.

Indeed, this is only a parable. All human knowledge is from some particular stand-point, and its view is limited by some particular horizon. The most ample descriptions do not convey all that may be seen; and the most profound and varied reflections never exhaust any great subject of thought. Personality is a marked factor of knowledge; personal peculiarities color it, and personal imperfections condition it. Our powers are few in number, limited in range, feeble in action, and fettered by habits.

Witnesses before juries often testify, with utmost sincerity, in a contradictory way, to facts of which they have all been equally cognizant. And even among practiced observers, like variations in accounts of natural phenomena occur. It is common for astronomers and microscopists to delineate precisely the same object, with such difference in description as to produce in the helpless listener's mind utter confusion. There are not two artists in the world that can paint the same landscape, so as to produce like pictures.

Literature has given us few dramatists and historians, because men can not readily free themselves from personal prepossessions, and take a foreign stand-point. To be able to see with other eyes, and to feel in emotions prompted by other than our own surroundings, is genius of a high sort.

And not only individuals are thus limited. Communities, races and ages have their common point of view and common horizon. The Greeks, incapable of appreciating merit other than their own, called alien races barbarians. The Chinese have done the same. Even to-day the Italians speak of foreigners as "forestieri," or savages. The Eskimo call themselves "the people," as do other isolated races. And, speaking of the Eskimo, one is reminded that, to them, Heaven is below in the warm regions of the under-earth, and the saints go down; while Hell is above in the icy chill of the upper air, and the wicked go up. In general, Hell is fiery to peoples living amid fierce heats, and icy to peoples suffering from endless winter. Just so, Satan is pictured by white races as black, and by black races as white.

Stand-point involves horizon; and it is curious to note how, as the eye of any individual or race or age looks out from things near and distinct to the Outermost Rim of the visible, it is found that thought becomes ever more and more feeble.

As we approach the limits of our intelligence on any side, thinking becomes difficult, and hence, often flaccid and indifferent,—the eye directing itself toward the horizon, sees blended together, indistinguishably, things small and great—a mountain, a lake, a cloud, and the wing of a bird.

A good illustration of this difficulty attending knowledge on the outermost limits is had in the indifference with which even thinking men receive the great recent discovery, by the spectroscope, of our chemical elements in the sun and stars. Consider what this involves and suggests.

The gases and solids of the earth are to be found in the sun and stars. The elements of which our atmosphere, our oceans, and our continents are composed, form the substance of the whole material creation. Notwithstanding the inconceivable distances and undoubted diversities of infinite space, there is oneness in substance as well as unity in law.

This discovery revives the old speculation about other worlds. We now recognize the possibility of other globes, containing forms of life similar, or at least allied to, those of earth. Doubtless they are remote. It may be that there is not another inhabitable globe within our solar system. Our planets are in general too old or too young for organic existence. Our own moon is without an atmosphere, burnt out —a cinder, as it has been termed—cold and dead. Jupiter, on the other hand, is yet in its early youth, still a molten ball, and not sufficiently cooled at the surface to offer a solid crust for life. Mars may perhaps provide the necessary conditions, and also, possibly, the moons of Jupiter and Saturn.

But the condition of our solar system does not at all affect the problem of a multiplicity of worlds. It is enough that there is one inhabitable globe. For there is an infinity of systems, and if these average even less than one such orb, it follows that there are an infinity of worlds. If there be but one inhabited globe in each solar system, or but one in ten systems, then are there, by virtue of a stupendous but inevitable sequence, earths teeming with life, infinite in number. As we look out upon the starry heavens, though there may, in the silence of the night, seem loneliness, the imagination is fairly entitled to picture universal existence —life infinitely distributed and infinitely diversified.

Yet how little does this tremendous possibility affect our imaginations, enter into our conversation, or even at all occupy our thoughts! How many even of very intelligent men, as they walk under the shining canopy of a star-lit night, find their thoughts going out into the measureless to picture other worlds and races; how many find any chord of sympathy touched by possibilities of non-human intelligences, achievements and virtues? Not one in a thousand, and with these not on one of a hundred nights.

We naturally think most often and most

clearly about matters that intimately concern us. Food, dress, friendship, the family, politics and similar affairs occupy our time and strength.

We are quite content to leave the heavens to astronomers; and the majesty of the universe, if we confess it, is rather painful, for the very strain it puts upon our faculties; and, if there be other inhabited worlds, their condition is too hopelessly unknown and unknowable to stimulate more than a passing curiosity.

It never is difficult to reach the limit of human thought in any given direction, and to draw visibly against the skies the Outermost Rim of vision—the horizon of knowledge. And, then, one is seen standing like Columbus on the shore of an unexplored ocean, wondering what beauty and life may be beyond.

For outside of the Outermost Rim of human thought, there is yet an infinity of truth—of things that are knowable, when the adequate powers of discovery and comprehension come to us. The mind's knowledge is like the eye's landscape: the eye sees what of the landscape comes within the power and sweep of vision, but beyond, unseen, roll away the mountains and the valleys, the rivers and the plains. So mental vision has its scope. Beyond the range of even poet's and prophet's insight, the endless world of knowledge rolls on and on.

CHAPTER II.

WIDENING HORIZONS.

"*The thoughts of men are widened, with the process of the suns.*"—TENNYSON.

THERE is an old Greek proverb, which declares that "man is the measure of the universe." It were better to compare him to one that wearily ascends the mountains with ever-widening horizons. He measures the universe only as the eye measures distance. The keener the eye and the higher the altitude, the more is there to measure.

The Outermost Rim of human thought is not fixed, neither for the race as a whole, nor for any individual. One man's horizon is another's foreground. Some are keener in sight than others, and some higher up. There is a wide band of knowledge between the Outermost Rim—of the savage, for instance, and the mental scope of the philosopher; between the thoughts of the dullard and of the genius. At any one time, in any great city, may be seen, as the eye scans the face of human society, the widening scope of vision, from the ignorant puzzle-headed churl of the slums to the white-haired gold-spectacled sage of the study, the laboratory and the rostrum.

Here is a savage—a South Sea Islander, let us suppose—whose world is a forest, whose sky is a brazen dome, his stars fire-flies hung against a canopy, his God a hulking spirit of childish malignity. This wretch has buried alive his aged mother, because her teeth were gone and she was become useless to herself and her tribe; he has slain his girl-babies, because unable to hunt, fish, and fight. He can not count ten: he can not form abstract conceptions: he can not reason consecutively on any given topic. He is a feebly-thinking animal.

Much higher stands the barbarian, with his house and his horse, his flexible language, his laws, his government, and his crude but unfolding intelligence. His world is a continent, his heaven at least a mystery, his Gods the forces of nature.

Higher still, we find the semi-civilized and the civilized spreading over a hemisphere, covering the seas with the white wings of commerce, adorning the land with cities, palaces, temples—the heavens a profound study for philosophers, religion a grand ceremonial, and deity becoming dim, vast and majestic.

At last our eye rests on the poet, the prophet,

the scientist of enlightenment; and lo! the skies are now the infinite expanse of flaming suns and of numberless planets, teeming with wondrous forms of life. The world is but a tiny globe, and God is the Creator, the Designer, and the Aim of All, through all and in all. From the notion of Deity has been eliminated all that can belittle Absolute Power and Infinite Wisdom and Goodness.

And this difference in horizons, to-day, is but the result of different rates of enlargement in days gone by. From the savage to the sage is not only a present contrast, but a movement of history. The savage of the 19th century is but an instance of arrested development.

No intelligent man, in these times, ought to deny a general onward and upward movement in human affairs. The river of progress is, indeed, unequal in its flow: here it frets its banks and there it dashes against rocks, while yonder it glides along, placid and deep; now it widens into a broad and shallow lake, and loiters over its rolling sands, and scarce can push through its rushes and lilies; now it hides behind bluffs and pauses in quiet coves, ere long, in narrow defiles, to dash forward impetuous and resistless; it has its surface ripples which run with the wind, it has its surface eddies which return on themselves, it has its under-currents, that the eye perceives not at all; but, slow or fast, noisy or still, it flows on and on, from its fountain in the primeval fire-mist to its Ocean of Eternity. The crudest notions of early ages and of unripe civilizations were pebble shocks on the surface of this river; that, as they became by ever-enlarging ripples a mighty circumference of deduction and inference, were themselves swept onward to mingle with the other forces of movement. The late Dr. James Martineau declared in one of his profound discourses: "Every fiction that has ever laid strong hold on human belief is the mistaken image of some great truth, to which reason will direct its search, while half-reason is content with laughing at the superstition, and unreason with believing it." The great thought of each after age was once a mere childish puzzling. As civilization progresses conceptions ripple out. One man sees, and he shows many men.

All great discoveries of underlying laws have come as a rise in altitude and a widening of horizon. The wise, by some new brilliancy of imagination, by some unwonted grasp of reason, discern and declare. The history of mathematics is of intense interest to us here. All its intricate methods and wonderful combinations have come by fresh unfoldings of intuition in certain select minds, which they themselves have been unable to explain. Simply they have risen higher, and see what others can not. They show other select minds—as it were, take them up the Mount of Vision, and these see; but generations pass ere such abstruse discoveries can be taught in the schools. The laws detected by a few, by and by form part of the education of all. The rare exotic becomes a garden vegetable—at first furnishing delight for the few, at last supplying food for all.

Thus, the discovery of fluxions by Newton, and of calculus by Leibnitz, has opened endless vistas of mathematical accomplishment. The establishment of the Copernican System lifted astronomy out of the region of ever-failing hypothesis into the position of an exact science, and guaranteed swift discovery. The demonstration of the laws of gravity by Newton did the same for mechanics, and prepared the way for all the recent discoveries in light, heat, electricity, and motion, viewed as expressions of force.

Music has advanced by leaps. At first, when Miriam fingered her lyre by the Red Sea, and David sang sweet psalms to the harp, music, whether instrumental or vocal, was but a melody—a simple succession of notes, with little that would be pleasing to the modern taste in the air; while instruments were of rudest construction. When Moses came down from the Mount, it was not strange that Joshua, hearing a hideous outcry among the tents, should have said, "There is a noise of war in the camp!" The people were singing; and even to Joshua, the man of battles, it seemed like the hoarse roar of infuriated combatants.

Harmony, or the combination of simultaneous tones, appeared not earlier than the Middle Ages, and at once attained a high degree of perfection; while orchestration, or the use in combination or in contrast, of instruments of different capacities and qualities of tone, was the product of the last century. About the middle of the last century, music underwent a wonderful illumination. A musician of rarest genius appeared, and in a succession of the most wonderful compositions the world had yet listened to, revolutionized the art, and ushered in an entirely new era. Mozart was a man of weak will, and the almost passive channel of ideas that came to him without effort, and of heavenly strains that wafted through his soul by day and by night. Nor was he alone. An angel chorus was come again to earth to make the Old World young. And with Mozart, and Haydn, and Handel, and Mendelssohn, and Beethoven, came oratorios and symphonies, so seraphic, so exalting, so beyond all former conception, that it has taken the gross world a century to recognize the sublimity of this outburst of art, of this enlarging of the range of the human mind and of the sphere of human happiness.

Such an outburst of genius gave us the Gothic cathedrals; and earlier a similar advance upon former art produced Italian painting, or still earlier, Grecian sculpture.

The beauties of nature are of recent discernment. The ancients did not keenly perceive the picturesque in landscape. The picturesque in action is delineated on their vases, walls, temples and tombs. Homer dwells fondly upon scenes of life action and passion; a lion aroused from his lair and tossing the dogs aside to dash at the hunter, a warrior going forth to battle in brazen armor, the sun glittering on his shield, a personal combat, a hive of bees, a council of war, a home circle, a storm at sea—such pictures are drawn with matchless art; but the beauty of mist and shadow and varying tints—what may be called the atmospheric charm of nature—wholly escaped him. As late as the last century, Oliver Goldsmith, who wrote the sweetest, purest English of his time, the versatile genius who at once composed an immortal novel, an immortal poem, and an immortal play, declared of the Scottish Highlands

— then given over to wild clans, but now thronged with tens of thousands of tourists, entranced with beauty of mountain and of lake — that they were "a hideous wilderness." "Everywhere the country presents the same dismal aspect!" And Samuel Johnson asserted that "country gentlemen could not be happy: there was not enough to keep their lives in motion."

At present the picturesque in Nature is dwelt upon with ardor, and its delineation has become an eminent part of successful art, whether for the painter, the poet, or the novelist.

Indeed, there seems not only a progress of thought in human history, but also a progress of thinking. There is reason to believe that the human mind is not only constantly developing its possibilities in various lines of advancement, but that also the brain, the organ of mind, is itself undergoing a change that multiplies its possibilities.

Does this seem improbable? But why should the Outermost Rim of even mental capacity be fixed?

Study for a moment the comparative anatomy of the nerve-centers of animals, and see what we shall learn, at least of the possibilities of improvement in the mental mechanism.

The lowest of creatures have no nervous

system; hence in them we discover no signs of any self-conscious intelligence. But early in the series nerve-cells appear, as in the lower of the mollusks. Here we find a mere beginning, with a simple arrangement of excitor and motor nerves. Rising higher, we find composite animals, each segment supplied with such an apparatus. Then we come to animals having heads and two or more ganglia furnishing a feeble brain for the exercise of vision and hearing, and perhaps of taste and smell. Still farther up the scale, there is discovered a spinal cord, or continuous aggregate of nerve-centers. Then, the spinal cord enlarges in the head of still higher creatures into ganglionic masses. We are now on the high-road of intelligence, and each rise in order brings us to a larger and finer brain, new masses of ganglia overlapping the old—to the spinal cord there is added a sensorium, to the sensorium a cerebellum, and to the cerebellum at last that final triumph of nature, the cerebrum—the organ of reason, of science, and of civilization.

Did I say final?

Who knows if the present man be the final product of Nature's marvellous fertility? Who knows what higher orders are possible, and perhaps somewhere existent? Who knows what may come to man as he is of new development? The future may not bring to the human head nerve masses to overlap the cerebrum; but it is very certain that the human brain, in the progress of civilization, has enlarged in average weight and size, and become more and more complex in convolution and nerve-branchings. No one can deny that the demands of enlightenment are answered by the development of new capabilities at the plastic nerve-centers. The study of nerve development furnishes prophecy of what shall be, of what even now may be in other worlds—explanation, encouragement, incitement.

Or leaving physiology, approach from the psychological stand-point. Watch the mental growth of a child. Every day you see the circle of thought widened, the altitude higher, the horizons broadening. You see, little by little, the clouds break, the mists dissolve, the heavens open, the stars shine, the universe revealed. Gaze into the bright, puzzled little eyes, as great thoughts appear on the Outermost Rim, like ships at sea out of the far-away horizon. The feeble reasonings would discern and understand, but can not. Do you not know that the man shall master what balks the child? And the greatest problems that defy the powers of the wisest men are but child's play; and these men are but babes to the sages that shall come.

And so we are brought to a position of supreme importance. If all human knowing has its limit, if the Outermost Rim is not fixed, if horizons forever expand, then knowledge is not final—it is relative, tentative, partial. "Now we know in part," quoth Paul.

Nay, it is no sacrilege to ascribe limits to even the highest conceivable modes of existence and to the loftiest beings, that may somewhere dwell. If there be angels and archangels, they penetrate not into all knowledge. Surely, for highest Principality and Heavenly Power there is an horizon—and Infinity Beyond!

Only an Absolute Intelligence has no Outermost Rim and no Beyond.

CHAPTER III.

THE MYSTERY OF NATURE.

> "*Race after race, man after man,*
> *Have thought that my secret was theirs,*
> *Have dreamed that I lived but for them,*
> *That they were my glory and joy;*
> *They are dust, they are changed, they are gone,*
> *I remain!"* —MATTHEW ARNOLD.

SEARCH Nature in what direction we may, we soon find our thought on the Outermost Rim. She shows us her waves, and their glancing lights and endless changes of form, but they only conceal her profound ocean.

The Cause, the Method, and the Purpose of Nature are each profoundly mysterious. Why? How? and by Whom? We may penetrate a little way into the fog, but soon are lost. We may say of rain that it is caused by certain electric and atmospheric conditions precipitating the moisture of the air; but immediately we ask, What made the moisture, and what guarantees the working of the conditions? We may assert evolution of Nature's progress, and think to have proven many interesting facts of method; but the moving force, the real evolver, is still hidden in Nature's background. And when we ask why this or that adaptation should occur, while we perceive Reason *in* it, we may utterly fail to find reasons *for* it. And Nature, as a whole, is a yet greater mystery even than any of its items.

Its mystery enlarges into the Infinite, and diminishes into the Infinitesimal.

Let us proceed to some details.

It would be easy here to weary the reader with the oft-stated astronomical magnitudes of the universe, and the infinities and infinitesimals of physics and mechanics.

One instance will suffice. A ray of light travels from the sun—upwards of ninety millions of miles—in less than ten minutes. Yet a ray from the polar star, moving with equal speed, requires forty-six years for its journey. And the polar star is a next-door neighbor.

We may find more novel and quite as profitable illustrations of Nature's mystery on every side.

Indeed, more wonderful far than even the celestial physics and mechanics are the facts of *life*. To these, for the moment, let us turn our attention.

Ultimately, life is the property of a vital jelly called protoplasm. For plant and for animal, existence at first is just one infinitesimal droplet of living slime; and if modern scientists are to be believed, existence at its genealogical beginning was just this,—only this, and nothing more.

Only this? Nay, now we use the language of ignorance. A drop of protoplasm is infinitely more marvellous than any or all of man's erections and contrivances, more marvellous than glaciers, than mountains, than bowling planets and flaming suns! And, being the starting-point of higher forms of life, the protoplasmic droplet is very naturally itself the lowest form of life.

In any stagnant water you may find Amœba—a sluggish mass of moving jelly, invisible to the naked eye, and, under the microscope, without form, without organs, without members. An unsightly mass, it pushes forward its substance in a blunt finger, and then—cankerworm-like—draws itself onward, though without eyes, feet, or muscles, rolling across the field, a vital motion of colorless slime. Sometimes the effort is too great for its cohesiveness; and then the two parts, the finger forward and the mass behind, separate. And then there are two creatures instead of one. It approaches a savory diatom. Behold the wise jelly flow up against its prey, ooze about the diatom, surround it, embrace it, and, by some mysterious chemistry, solve out the edible portion within, soon to flow away onward anywhither, leaving the crystal shell behind.

Growth is but a multiplication, by division and absorption, of an original protoplasmic droplet. The lichen that colors the rock, the alga thrown out upon the sea-beach of the storm-tide, the annual that blossoms in our gardens, the shrubs and fruit-trees that crowd our gardens and orchards, and the leafy giants that lift proud heads toward the skies in our forests, all are but multiplications of an original cell.

Animal growth is similar. Even our human bodies are, in all their parts, the result of cell division and cell manufacture, and, indeed, may be looked upon as an assemblage—infinite in number and greatly diversified in appearance and function—of cells and their products. Man, as a living thing, is a polypidom. Many of his composite cells have a comparatively independent existence. During a violent cold, living cells, abundantly provided with cilia, very active and capable of lively motion, are dislodged from the mucous coating of the nasal passages, and discharged in the catarrhal flow; and the microscopist may behold part of himself, as independently existent, for the moment, as any animalcule. Living cells often survive the death of the body as a whole; and the reason that death reduces all to corruption in a short time is probably, that the individual cells perish for lack of nourishment.

Over the porch of the author's parsonage there droops a Virginia creeper, on the leaves of which, any day in summer, may be found tiny yellowish pellets, resembling drops of amber. Gather some of these. Now go down to yonder lake, and from the under-side of overturned stones in the shallow water of the shore, you shall find little masses of dotted slime as large as a pea. Secure two such masses, and observe that the dots are white pellets. Examine the white and the yellow pellets day by day with a microscope. The pellets are simple cells, and no great difference is apparent between the three kinds. To-day each is only a little protoplasm, confined by a thin membrane. To-morrow we shall find a division of contents, and two cells in each pellet; and day after to-morrow four, and the next day eight. Complexity will increase, until we become quite confused by indefinite lines and curves. But, in the end, there shall be a recognizable form, a movement, and at last rupture of the covering membrane. We shall then perceive that our amber pellets are become each a beautiful insect, that the droplets of the first mass of slime are changed into snails, and the droplets of the second mass into fresh-water lobsters. From three simple and similar specks of living jelly will have come insects, mollusks, and crustaceans. This same study of embryology we might carry through the whole animal kingdom, always beginning with a cell and always ending with some one of Nature's animated creatures. Protoplasm never makes any mistakes: it ever works true to its idea. It commences in seeming identity: it ends in all the diversity of the sea-bottoms and the forests.

The cell is Nature's laboratory: here she generates organic substances—starch, sugar, gluten, oil, and, no doubt, in animals, vital forces. The worker is protoplasm.

If one will cut a section of any living vegetable tissue, and examine it with the microscope, the cells are seen crowding one another, and, through their transparent walls, the operations of vitality in full effort. So small are these tiny chambers that a hundred millions of them would not fill a cubic inch measure. They appear as compartments, closed in on every side, yet not hermetically sealed. The walls are porous, and juices freely may flow through the entire tissue. The protoplasm—chemist, manufacturer, life-giver—lies just inside this bibulous membrane, in a thin lining; it is also distributed through the chamber in threads and small masses. Between these threads and masses, in the spaces remaining, may be seen the products of activity,—the cell-sap, and floating in this, starch grains, oil globules, crystals, crystalloids, and living cell-germs which frisk about in all the sportiveness of youth. Most important is a denser portion of the protoplasm, called the nucleus, in which the power of self-division and multiplication lies.

The protoplasm itself, is a soft, tough, inelastic, extensible body; which, to the chemist, displays only simple elements, combined together apparently in a commonplace albuminous substance; yet, as we have seen, it turns out, with ease and the most perfect precision, compounds that baffle the skill of the greatest chemists, and, unseen and noiseless, weaves all the wondrous fabric of life.

But enough upon the mere phenomena of life and growth. Proceeding to the study of the higher and more complicated forms of vitality, our attention at every step is directed to marvels most astonishing.

On the shores of many ponds and swamps is found the pitcher-plant. It has neither brains nor nerves, and yet embodies a device which can furnish us abundant substance for reflection.

It is remarkable for its leaf, which is a hollow, trumpet-shaped tube, with an over-arching hood. The tube is half-filled with water, which the leaf itself has secreted and which is befouled with the hard parts of flies and insects. In short, the leaf is a trap: in its water, insects are drowned and their softer parts dissolved, to be absorbed into the tissues as nutriment. The pitcher-plant is carnivorous, and thrives on animal diet.

But how does a vegetable growth entice its animal prey into a watery grave? It can not, like the swallow, catch them on the wing. It can not, like a spider, bind them with silken cords in the meshes of a web. None of the devices of conscious ingenuity would seem open to its choice. Yet, unconscious and unthinking, without action and without feeling, it selects the very wisest of means to attain its end. Sarracenia fills her larder by the agency of a large number of tiny glands at the throat of her tube, which secrete a sweet fluid, enticing to ants and flies. This lures the victim downward. Pursuing his honeyed way, the intruder passes over a multitude of long, sharp spines, which, pointing downward, offer no obstacle to descent. And now he stands on the brink of the deadly well, full of the remains of former victims. Would he retreat: above him hang down the spines (possibly poisoned) pointing full at him—a formidable abattis, which he can neither force nor surmount. It results that he dies in the plant and furnishes a rich feast.

Now, who or what has thought out all this subtle contrivance, and why? Surely not the pitcher-plant itself. Was it created with a taste for animal food, with its glands and its bristles, and its pool of death? or did it, in the struggle for existence, through favorable variations and survival of the fittest, come to be thus thrifty? In either case the mystery is profound. If specific creation wrought the wonder, the mystery is truly colossal; if natural selection is to be credited, no less are we astonished, and we must continue to ask, whose wit proposed the condition of a law resulting thus shrewdly? What or who was interested; that Sarracenia should vary her diet of minerals and gases with animal food. Ah! we are on the Outermost Rim and looking far over Beyond—and beyond is Mystery!

And only seemingly less wonderful than the craft of Sarracenia, is the wit of a spider which infests a pitcher-plant of Florida, who hides himself under the hood, and there exacts from the incoming procession of flies and ants, tribute of such juicier ones as please his fancy; or the cunning of an ant in Borneo, which, having discovered the danger of entering Sarracenia from the top, tunnels up from the bottom through the stalk and greedily devours her entire store.

If the reader has ever walked on an ocean beach, he has thoughtlessly trodden on small flattened balls, empty within, and covered with spines without. These are dead sea-urchins; which, when living, moved over the shallow sea-bottoms; and which, now dead and emptied of the flesh within, the tide has tossed out upon the sands. Take one up, and look well at its perforated shell-case and at its ugly bristles. You say, "It is not so beautiful as a boy's agate marble, and not near so intricate as a French clock or a Dresden music-box." Ah! is it not! Then shut the eye of sense and look with the eye of science. You can read the secret of the clock or of the music-box, even with your eye of sense; and the ingenuity once mastered, you shall soon come down to raw brass and steel. But even the eye of science will fail to solve the secret of this sea-urchin. You may muse upon it a thousand years and not get behind its veil of mystery. The secret of the universe is in it.

This globular shell, it is really three hundred

plates of shell, deftly cemented together. Nay, it is not shell at all, but rather an airy lace-work of calcareous fibre, porous as blotting-paper. And these two thousand spines that beset the surface, and give it so formidable an aspect: take but a magnifying-glass and you shall find them tall elegant columns, tapering upward and fluted like the pillars of some old Grecian temple. Indeed, under the microscope, this rough exterior becomes the ruins of a Doric temple, the columns lying one upon another in the confusion of some earthquake-shaken ancient site.

Cut a thin section directly across one of these fluted pillars, and examine the structure within. Before you is a very beautiful object, ring within ring: first, a ring of marble disks, and then a ring of lace-work—marble disks and lace-work from circumference to hollow center, all tinged with rich purple. The column is a series of cylinders—of rods alternating with lace-work.

These columns are, in a sense, legs for the urchin, at their base shapen into cups, and fitting exactly upon spherical knobs on the shell, upon which by ball-and-socket movement they are worked by powerful muscles. Moreover, there are ten rows of minute perforations in the shell-case, making in all several thousand tiny pin-holes, from which, when the animal is alive, long flexible members are protruded, some with an elegant disk of marble lace-work for adhesion, and others with powerful jaws for seizure.

In short, the odd little sea-urchin, crawling over the shallow marine bottoms, feeding on corallines and shell-fish, hints at far more than is arrived at in the philosophy of the wisest of us. How did all this prodigality of beauty and of marvel come about? Whose thought does it utter, and for what purpose?

The microscopic anatomy of the human body is full of surprises for us.

Every time one enjoys a sunset, as the gaze rests for a moment upon the setting orb, a ray of light enters the eye. But imagine the speed of its introduction. For each second of such vision, a beam of sunshine 190,000 miles long slides into the eye-ball, and discharges itself upon the retina. This beam is a vibration of ether (?) and enters the organ of sight in the form of waves and breaks upon the retina, as the ocean upon the sea-shore, in a sort of ethereal surf. During one second of vision, not less than five hundred millions of millions of light waves dash into the eye and beat against its breastwork of nerves. And this breastwork of nerves is composed (according to Salzer) of 438,000 fibers and 3,360,000 cones.

A bundle of human muscle no thicker than a little finger is composed of at least fifteen thousand fibers, each with its own arteries and nerves. Every one of these fibers is itself a strand composed of thousands of minute fibrils; while each fibril is a roll of disks, of which there are seventeen thousand to the inch. And, for all we know to the contrary, each of these infinitesimal disks may be a whole world of complexity, variety, and beauty. A bundle of muscular fiber one inch long and half an inch in diameter will thus contain about 15,000 fibers, 30,000,000 fibrils, and 510 billions of disks, not to speak of the capillary vessels and nerves, that feed and control all this wonderful machinery.

Every time one breathes, over five hundred millions of air-cells are inflated, and five hundred millions of networks of capillary vessels send their blood-disks along, purified, vitalized, dancing for joy.

Such statements might be continued until the reader wearied of magnitudes and incomprehensibilities. The telescope and the microscope only push out the Outermost Rim; they leave infinite mystery beyond on every side.

Or if, leaving the outer world, we look within, and study that mind which, as Wordsworth says,

>"Builds for aye,"

there is no release for astonishment.

What is this intelligence that flashes from the eye, and on the tongue vocalizes itself in uttered thought? What is this taste that devises images of beauty, and clothes the world with pleasing contrast and harmony, and finds in the story of man material for comedy and tragedy? What is this wild throbbing of the heart, this weariness, this despair, this hope and ambition, this hate, this love?

And when Death lays his chill hand upon this frame, and the body lies stiff and cold, whither has flown intelligence and taste and emotion? Where now is the glorious flash of the eye, the ardent curvings of the lips, and all the lines and graces of vital motion inspired of thought and robed in beauty. Alas! hushed are the winged words—

>"Life and thought have gone away side by side,
>Leaving door and windows wide,
>Careless tenants they!"

O mystery fathomless! And, like the living cell, comparatively unexplored; for every age shows man to himself a more wonderful creation. As Pope wisely wrote, "The proper study of mankind is man." Go to the libraries, visit the picture-galleries, scan human society, review human history, look into your own soul, and ponder perception and memory and imagination and desire and conscience and will, hope and fear, love and hate! Is not intelligent existence the snow-white peak of Nature's loftiest pinnacle? Forgetting here aught else, we are tempted to adopt Sir W. Hamilton's lecture-room motto, and to say, "There is nothing great in the world but man, and nothing great in man but mind."

Consider, for instance, that very wonderful fact, noticed by all thoughtful men, that many of the most valuable of our mental results can not be traced back to any conscious act of knowledge, to any conscious process of reasoning, or to any conscious outburst of artistic frenzy. There seems at times to work within us a lawless imagination—a sort of demoniac artist, that paints without materials, without effort, and with results often of surpassing brilliancy. There is a discernment of facts which apparently have not been learned, a divination of future contingencies or a solution of problems which seems without explanation and akin to the insight of the seer, or some strange and wonderful combination of fictitious elements into dramatic pose, flashing on the soul like a vision of revelation. Thus suddenly will be thrown upon the mental canvas, from some invisible stereopticon, a fact or event of which the mind has no conscious memory. We say to ourselves, this surely is but some figment of fancy, a fragment of some day-dream; yet it is vivid enough to be true. And, sure enough, by and by it proves to have occurred. The mind, by some hidden process, had taken knowledge of what never came into consciousness; and now the fact which thus had stolen into memory comes forth with boldness. Reasoning processes of the most elaborate kind will go on without any consciousness of them, and suddenly the mind has accepted of conclusions which seem utterly bereft of premises,—foundlings that no mental effort will own. Problems that puzzle will suddenly lose their obscurity; and there will appear on the mental blackboard the solution clearly chalked out. Says O. W. Holmes: "I question whether persons who think most— that is, have most conscious thought pass through their minds — necessarily do most mental work. The tree you are sticking in will be growing when you are sleeping. So with every new idea that is planted in a real thinker's mind: it will be growing when he is least conscious of it. An idea in the brain is not a legend carved on a marble slab: it is an impression made on a living tissue, which is the seat of active nutritive processes. Shall the initials I carved in bark increase from year to year with the tree? and shall not my recorded thought develop into new relations with my growing brain?"

Very many of the greatest discoveries of science or of the most wonderful inventions of mechanics have come thus as images, long ere proved to be correct by evidence. The mind, outrunning the slow course of investigation, has worked out the result, ere even the thinker,—much less the thinking world in general,—has been able to convince himself of its soundness. Much of what we call insight into character, forecast of the future, business capacity, judgment, common sense, intuition, tact and taste, is simply this automatic working of the mind, which hides its processes and reveals only its results. And demonology of old found a stronghold, and now has explanation, in this occult mental activity.

This unconscious cerebration has been beautifully likened to the "innumerable waves that travel by night, unseen and in silence, over the broad expanse of an ocean. Consciousness may bear some analogy to the sheen and roar of the breakers, where a single line of waves is lashed into a foam on the shores that obstruct their course."

And is it not a wonderful ocean, whether calm or disturbed, whether silent or in uproar, in darkness or broken into white foam,—this "vasty deep" of the human mind?

CHAPTER IV.

THE WORLD'S SHADOW.

> "*We look before and after,*
> *And pine for what is not;*
> *Our sincerest laughter*
> *With some pain is fraught;*
> *Our sweetest songs are those*
> *That tell of saddest thought.*"
> —SHELLEY.

NEARLY two thousand years ago, in one of the most lovely landscapes on earth, there rose a proud Roman city. The blue ocean in the foreground approached almost near enough to wash its walls; and behind its gates and towers arose a verdure-clad mountain. To right and left the green shores came out to sea and formed a picturesque bay. Far away through the summer haze were to be discerned the dreamy outlines of hills. Villas, embowered in the gray foliage of olives and in the lustrous dark green of orange and lemon groves, lined the shores. Vineyards climbed the slopes and to the very mountain-peak, and gardens luxuriated in the seldom-interrupted sunshine of perpetual summer. A river, fed by fountains back among the hills, flowed through the dense vegetation and babbled by the city's walls.

Probably a more calm and beautiful landscape was not to be seen of mortal eyes on all the earth. And the people of Pompeii were serene on that day, and the gay city was all out in gala dress. Business was suspended, save only employment of necessary provision. The public ovens were filled with bread; the wine-shops were open for tardy countrymen strolling in; women and children were, in many instances, in the tessellated courts of their houses, seated beside the fountain and under the silken awning; while at the open gates stood soldiers with sword and spear. But the great mass of the inhabitants, both men and women, gentry and mob, were seated on the stone benches of the amphitheatre, eagerly following the murderous strokes of gladiators, who fought in the oval arena below. Except for the wretches who were dying upon the bloody sands, it was a scene of gay costume, merry banter and general festivity.

Suddenly there was a sound of gurgling in the throat of the green mountain, a cloud passed over the sun, the heavens blackened into midnight; and there came down upon the city a shower of sulphur and ashes. And then fell burning cinders of molten stone, a storm of fire-flakes penetrated by rocky hail.

Forth from the great amphitheatre, through its many openings for exit, streamed the terrified crowd. Some hurried to the gates and to the sea-shore: some stopped to find their children in their burning homes: some delayed to seize the precious things long since hoarded away. Many died, suffocated or burned to death, in the streets. Whole families were entombed alive in their own vaults. Here sinks the priest, who, having cut his way through two solid walls, perishes ere he can open the third. See this wretch, as he falls back upon the pavement of the street, clutching his bag of gold and silver coins; that doubtless has stayed his flight, and so robbed him of his life. And here, in the beautiful house of the poet, whose walls are so superbly frescoed in elegant designs, behold these dainty ladies that care more for adornment than for safety, and who stop to gather up their jewels, and in the effort die. In this wine-cellar of the rich Diomed, women and children, clasped into one another's arms, breathe out their last in statuesque horror. The mule in the bakery, the horses in the tavern, this goat with bell on his collar that has vainly thrust its head into an opened oven to escape the tempest of fire, and yonder prisoners in the pillory, perish not more helplessly. And see this mother clutching her babe to her bosom and huddling into a tomb, only to be walled in by the ashes and rock. And then this hero at the Herculaneum gate, this sentinel brave and calm, that lowers not his proud head nor leaves his post, but dies on duty, erect, spear in hand.

And so Pompeii disappeared beneath the ashes of the great eruption, and grass and forest trees, and vineyards and olive-yards grew upon its site to mock its memory; until modern research, inquisitive to know all things, dug out its streets and courts, uncovered its painted walls, and brought to view the bones of its victims. And Pompeii, to-day, immortalized by destruction, welcomes every traveller to its ruins. The ruts in roadways, the crocks in wine-shops, the scribblings of boys upon the walls, the very bread from the public ovens burnt to charcoal, are all there for any one to see and ponder.

And Pompeii is not alone in its pitiful appeal to the reason and the heart. Indeed, we have recalled that day of horror, only because history and research have combined to make this particular picture of human woe vivid. Any one may take up the daily newspapers, and in oft-recurring conflagrations of theatres and hotels, in railroad collisions, and in disasters at sea, may read the same ghastly story of security, merriment, catastrophe and destruction, mocked by a hurried paragraph of description, and liable only, by chance, to the poor immortality of recollection among the future memories of mankind. And were great public disasters to fail, private sorrows innumerable,—pestilence ever lurking somewhere, and want, pain and death,—would call attention, with keenest emphasis, to the World's Shadow.

How many stories, like this that follows, voice the sadness of the human heart: A thousand years ago there lived in Persia a poet of genius, who, by his immortal verse, rose to the highest eminence. At the bidding of King Mahmoud he wrote a great epic "Book of Kings" of sixty thousand verses, for each verse of which he was to have in payment a gold piece. Firdousi was not covetous; and he longed only to be a public benefactor. It seems that his native town was subject to overflow. So he resolved to build a great dyke with his golden pieces; that all his fellow-citizens might share in his earnings, and bless his kind heart and open hand. So he labored in poverty and privation, refusing to receive any of the promised pay until all was earned. When, however, after years of supreme effort the work was done, Mahmoud repented of his generosity, and, instead of gold, sent silver to the poet. Firdousi was in the public bath when the elephant arrived that bore the three sacks of silver. On discovering the fraud, the great man's heart was broken, his dreams of public good dissolved; and, enraged beyond control, scornfully he gave one sack of treasure to the messenger that brought it, the second he bestowed on the bath-keeper, and the last he paid for a glass of beer. Then sending the false monarch a bitter rebuke in verse, he fled the land. Years went by. Long after, Mahmoud, his conscience ill at ease, forwarded an ample apology, a robe of honor and one hundred thousand pieces of gold, beseeching the poet to come back to his capital. But as the camels entered the city where Firdousi had found asylum at one gate, the funeral procession of the poet, dead of grief, was leaving the city by another.

And those who saw, said: "Vanity of vanities: all is vanity!" And all who read are tempted to murmur, with the poet's voice of doubt—

> "All things are shows,
> And vain the knowledge of their vanity;
> Thou dost but chase the shadow of thyself!
> Rise and go hence: there is no better way
> Than patient scorn;—nor any help for man!"

It is the fundamental doctrine of Buddhism, that life is an evil intolerable. The best gift virtue can confer upon a holy man is that, when he dies, he shall not be born again, but sink into blissful, unconscious, eternal sleep. "Anywhere, anywhere, out of the world," was for ages the cry of the holiest men of one of the greatest moral movements the world has ever seen.

It is significant that the poets, who, by reason of their genius, are gifted to drink most deeply of the wine of life, have very generally formed melancholy views of human existence. A whole volume of sadness is breathed into Shelley's couplet—

> "Life, like a dome of many-colored glass,
> *Stains* the white radiance of Eternity."

Even the gentle Longfellow sings mournfully—

> "Life hath quicksands,
> Life hath snares!"

To one bard, life's

> .... "A tale
> Told by an idiot, full of sound and fury,
> Signifying nothing."

It is "a cheat," "a dull round," "a span," "an empty dream," "a fitful fever," "tedious as a twice-told tale." These phrases are proverbial.

And must we conclude that man is the product and plaything of the gigantic forces of Nature, that now work in harmony to bring about beauty and joy, and ere long collide in terrific onset, in earthquakes, in pestilences, in the submersion of continents, and in the conflagration of worlds?

And is there no more of it? Is life only continuous sensation, troubled matter come to sorrowful consciousness,—momentary knowledge of a mystery incomprehensible? Is death the end of the wild drama? It was Coleridge who wrote the lines—

> "The stilly murmur of the distant sea
> Tells us of silence."

Can it be true that, after all, the rustle of life is but that stilly murmur of Eternity that tells of silence? Shall wit and wisdom offer no solace for human ills but the moan of the poet Moschus, as sweetly and sadly he chants his dirge over his brother-poet, Bion:

"Woe! woe! The mallows, when they perish in the garden, and the green parsley, and the blooming, crisp-leaved anise, after a season live again, and year by year they grow anew; but we—great and strong and wise men—when once we have died, we sleep forgotten in the hollowed earth, the long, long, endless sleep from which we never shall awake!"

PART II.

VOICES FROM BEYOND.

CHAPTER V.

HINTS OF GOD IN PHYSICAL NATURE.

"*He who will look steadfastly out into the world, will perceive himself surveyed by a great eye returning his stare.*"
—R. W. EMERSON.

THE reader's attention, in this chapter, is called to a vastly-important series of suggestions in the physical world, that urge the mind to contemplation of an Ultimate Thinker.

And, first, let it be carefully noted and mused upon, that in the study of Nature we discover a *thoughtfulness* like our own, though farther-reaching and superior.

This has been the constant, inevitable inference of all that we have shown in the first and interrogatory portion of this work. We have pondered upon inconceivable distances and rapidities, upon the marvels of growth, life and upon the play of organisms, and upon the intricacies of the human mind. We have seen that each science opens to view a whole universe of wonders, which at once expands into the infinite and diminishes into the infinitesimal. And we have found, not only an exclamation point over against every fact, but as well a mark of interrogation. Everywhere we have encountered thought, even in senseless plants, and we have puzzled ourselves with the question, Whose Thought? And we must have been forced again and again to the conclusion of James Martineau: " Unless it takes more mental faculty to construe a Universe than to cause it, to read the Book of Nature than to write it, we must more than ever look upon its sublime face as the living appeal of thought to thought!"

And if any now object to our applying a word descriptive of the mental processes to the mysterious Somewhat in Nature that causes and conditions, let it be further considered that human intelligence, studying the world, finds therein anticipated precisely *its own* thoughts.

All man's devices seem to have been anticipated, and long before there were any conscious thinkers.

To illustrate, take the vaunted triumphs of our mechanical skill. The workman justly is proud of his tool-chest, whereby the dexterity of his deft fingers is multiplied many times. But there is not one tool of them all that has not been somehow acquired by animated creatures. The *idea*, at least, of each kind of instrument has long ago been utilized by beetles, ants, butterflies and beasts small and great.

Monkeys made suspension-bridges, and ants dug tunnels and erected arched ways and domed houses, before ever a civilized man trod the earth.

The shipwright builds a vessel, and the mariner sails the Deep in proud consciousness of dominion over the physical world; does he reflect that, ages upon ages ago, the tiny argonaut glided over the waves in an airy skiff of pearl? Corrugated sheet-iron for cars and other purposes requiring combined strength and lightness, is a recent device; but in the body of the cuttle-fish, from the morning of time, just this principle, far more elegantly developed, secures these desirable qualities for a hard structure within serving for skeleton. The principle of the steam-engine,—fuel converted into power. —is the principle of all animated action in Nature—of walking, swimming, flying and working,—only the fuel with an animal is called food.

How inventors strain their resources and their

wits to fabricate a flying-machine: even the heavy goose mocks at them. A carrier-pigeon has been known to outspeed the swiftest express trains. What ingenuity has been expended upon the art of forcing water up to elevated positions. The suction-pump gives out at thirty-four feet above the well, and all other contrivances to supply its defects are simply methods of pushing the fluid up by main force. But the giant pines of California and the blue gum trees of Australia draw the sap from their roots up four hundred feet and more to their topmost twigs;—we have yet to learn how.

Agriculture is generally supposed to be a purely human art; yet there is a race of ants in Texas that prepares a plot of ground, and sows, cultivates and reaps a kind of grain.

As we have observed in our third chapter, even plants anticipate man's thoughts, quite as though possessed of consciousness. We entrap flies with honey. So does the Pitcher Plant, the Venus Fly-trap, and other similar growths. Our frontiersmen set gins, dig pits, and use various devices to secure game for their subsistence. These plants all are regular trappers, and live on their catches.

Turning from mechanical arts to our boasted fine arts, the general fact we are illustrating again vividly appears. The larks sang, and the violets bloomed, and the forests murmured and waved, and landscapes were beautiful and grand, and the stars made music in their spheres, when our ancestors were barbarians, seeing naught—hearing naught—of beauty. We ourselves are only,—like the merchant of the Arabian Nights in the palace,—getting our eyes used to the splendors of our surroundings. Well wrote Lamartine of the beautiful in art: "Man, after all rarely invents anything he remembers." Creative art is but unusual insight into Nature's lovelier thoughts, and skilful combination of them.

Or will we teach Nature our science? *Our* science! Nature knows it all, practices it all, and has laboratories and museums, lenses and scalpels. The chemist boasts to the skies if he succeed in making but one of those many organic substances—as sugar, starch or oil; which Nature, in her living cells, is manufacturing with greatest ease, precision and prodigality. The galvanic battery is a very great triumph of human ingenuity; yet most powerful batteries have been for ages actively at work in the Electric eel, in the Torpedo fish.

But it is not necessary farther to enlarge upon this fact. Physical Nature knows chemistry, mechanics, geometry, nay, all sciences and all practical and fine arts. And the wiser man grows the more will he become convinced that Nature is before him in all his thoughts; and, at last, he can only conclude that the summit of human science and art is, after all, but knowledge of Nature's alphabet.

It is, therefore, no stretching of inference to declare boldly that there is thought in the physical world, and of a character analogous, and yet superior, to man's. We may sing with a recent English poet:

"To sit on rocks, to muse on flood and fell,
   To slowly trace the forest's shady scene,
Where things that own not man's dominion dwell,
   And mortal foot hath ne'er or rarely been.
To climb the trackless mountain all unseen,
   With the wild flock that never needs a fold,—
Alone o'er steeps and foaming falls to lean,—
   This is not solitude; 'tis but to hold
   Converse with Nature's charms and view her stores unrolled."

There is no solitude in Nature, but voices many that challenge the intelligence of the loftiest minds and quicken the spirituality of the purest hearts.

But who or what is this Intelligence? What or who thinks these thoughts?

Are there not other hints in the physical world to qualify the Ultimate Thinker? There are several of great significance.

After the first astonishment consequent upon the discovery of one's own thoughts everywhere, the observant and pensive student of Nature perceives other great facts.

(2.) One finds *unbroken succession* in Nature. It is an old proverb which, while it explains nothing, at least states much, that "Nature abhors leaps."

We speak of months and years; but duration knows nothing of intervals. Time glides on and Nature glides on. We have our midnight and noon; but the sun nowhere begins and nowhere ends in its daily circuit. Sunrise for Boston or New York is sunset for Asia; sunset for Boston or New York is dawn over the Pacific. Our seasons mark no sudden transition. Nature, in her succession of seed-time, blossom-time and harvest, glides onward at her own chosen pace.

Even our years are purely conventional. No monument in space marks the arrival of our earth at any special turning-point in its orbit. The earth whirls forward in its circuit to-morrow as to-day, to-day as yesterday; and sun and planets roll on forever through space. Nothing is without cause, nothing without effect.

Human history has epochs, made by violent insurrections and revolutions; and we term these the beginnings of eras. But the sharpness of the turning-point is largely our own inability to grasp the causes in conjunction with the effects. Could the historian study the long details of preparation, he would find his epoch very much like other points of time, the logical consequent of what has gone before.

The science of geology is at present forcing the same facts upon our attention. Fifty years ago geologists insisted upon the most violent upheavals and disruptions as necessary to explain the record of the rocks in the story of the early prime, but to-day they ask rather for time. They find evidence to believe that the earth, during prehistoric ages, was subject to conditions similar, in the main, to those producing results to-day; and they admit that movements were then, as now, in unbroken sequence.

Thus æons, eras, centuries, years, months, days, hours and minutes are but the terms of our incapacity to grasp the whole of Nature's advance, words of convenience and usage, uttered from a human stand-point, to describe the seeming stages of Nature's ceaseless flow.

(3.) Moreover, there is observable in Nature

Persistency of Law. The same atoms, the same forces and identical laws prevail forever! Nature's sequence is not only unbroken, it is consistent with itself.

There is to-day on our Atlantic shores a species of bivalve belonging to a genus (Lingula) found in our oldest geological formations. When the world first emerged from chaos, on the pebbly sea-bottoms were shell-fish all but identical in form and manner of life with some that any child may to-day find on the sea-beaches after a storm. The author has in his mineralogical cabinet specimens of Isle La Motte Monumental—a dark marble from the Lower Silurian—which, when cut in sections for the microscope, is shown to be composed of water-worn tests of rhizopods and the hard parts of zoophytes, etc.; each tiny fossil suggestive of what any collector may find in the proper localities to-day. The conditions remaining the same, in these instances the type has persisted for millions of years. When sunlight first penetrated the primæval vapors to fertilize the earth, it travelled at the same swift speed as to-day. Heat, electricity, magnetism and gravity all obeyed the laws, which are now, one by one, revealing themselves to the patient discoverer. Through all these ages never an atom of any substance has increased or decreased in weight, never a force varied its mechanical equivalent, never a physical law failed of its working. There have been no mistakes, no reconsiderations, no abandonments, but inevitable relentless operation.

(4). Finally, Nature, in her successive forms, shows a *progress of thought.* While the atoms and the forces and the laws never vary, the resulting forms, infinitely manifold, rise with the ages in the scale of being. The ages, when we make them speak for themselves, in the record of the rocks or upon the pages of history, tell of a steady onward flow. This, in its general bearing upon an expanding human civilization, we have already, in the second chapter, amply enlarged upon. The fact concerns us, at this point, in its bearings upon the question of a Cause and its nature.

No intelligent man to-day questions the fact of some general progress of things in Nature and in History. The word most often on the lips of the scientist is that term which covers so much ignorance, and yet recalls such wondrous discoveries,—Evolution. Name the progress of life evolution, development or what you will, it is not fortuitous but methodical, the utterance of sublimest intelligence.

This progress of thought is not strictly consecutive, but, if we may use the figure, genealogical. The evolution or development or consecution of natural life has been much like the growth of a tree, at first a mere cell, and then a root and a trunk,—the trunk dividing into limbs, the limbs into branches, the branches into boughs, the boughs into stems and the stems into twigs. And this division has not been evenly, but according to advantage of position. Here and there a limb has died out, here and there a branch is more than commonly vigorous and yonder are stems that have been stunted; some boughs are in the sunshine and some in the shadow, some receive more sap than others, and some more heat, and some more moisture; and the best fruit may be on a lower limb. But, on the whole, the tree ever rises and ever divides, clearly showing a general progress.

Let us now recapitulate. We have found thought everywhere, and anticipations even of our own particular devisings. We have seen that events occur, with the physical world, in unbroken succession, and that Nature's laws are invariable and forever persistent, and furthermore that there is clearly manifest, with the roll of the ages, a progress of thought in the evolution of forms.

Must we not now conclude that the physical Universe is one and simple, and say with the poet:

"Yet I doubt not, through the ages one increasing purpose runs"?

And are we not forced to infer that the Thinker of Nature is One and Simple? And do we not learn that whatever and whoever the Ultimate Thinker may be, the workings of the Intelligence are consecutive, according to foreordained Law, and progressively unfolding—in short, rigidly methodical, and the method infinite in its reach and eternal in its persistency? So far, the Mystery of Nature is perfectly simple; and amid all the confusion of countless startling facts is heard at all times and everywhere a clear, loud voice from Beyond, proclaiming an Intelligent Thinker, over all, back of all and in all.

And we must muse with Wordsworth:

> "For I have learned
> To look on Nature, not as in the hour
> Of thoughtless youth, but hearing oftentimes
> The still sad music of humanity,
> Nor harsh nor grating, though of ample power
> To chasten and subdue. And I have felt
> A Presence, that disturbs me with the joy
> Of elevated thoughts, a sense sublime

Of something far more deeply interfused,
Whose dwelling is the light of setting suns
And the round ocean and the living air
And the blue sky and in the mind of man,
A motion and a spirit that impels
All thinking things, all objects of all thoughts,
And rolls through all things."

CHAPTER VI.

HINTS OF GOD IN THE MORAL NATURE OF MAN.

"*None can escape the Presence! The Ought is everywhere and imperative. Alike guilt in the soul and anguish in the flesh attest his ubiquity.*"—BRONSON ALCOTT.

IN the last chapter we listened to the Voices from Beyond, audible in Physical Nature. Let us now hearken to what of suggestiveness there may be in the *moral* nature of man.

The Ultimate Thinker has a witness in conscience, whose testimony is worthy of utmost respect; of whom, if we interrogate, we learn three great truths.

First, that men have a sense of right and wrong and form clear moral judgments. Certain kinds of action and certain states of mind, by a mental and moral necessity, range themselves under the ideas of right and wrong.

Not always, to be sure, correctly, not always consistently. Any particular judgment may be faulty, and two judgments may contradict one another; but the bare sense of moral quality is ever present.

Men and women are very near-sighted in questions of probity, and their judgments are apt to be biased by their interests; but even at their worst they are beings of moral perceptions. This is all that is claimed.

But this bare sense of right and wrong is a great advance, it will be noticed, upon the ideas of the physical world, and fairly lifts man into a kingdom by himself.

To be sure, there are some who urge an incipient moral sense for dogs, horses, apes and other intelligent animals, and who believe that these may, in some instances, have suffered virtuous remorse and shame. Possibly this may be the case; but, if so, such conscientiousness can scarcely be more than a faintest anticipation of what we find in man, and very much as the intelligence of the ant and the elephant foreshadow, in scarcely perceptible outlines, human philosophy and art. Undeniably the law of life for the brutes is the law of tooth and claw. To escape a stronger foe and to devour a weaker is the Golden Rule of beasts, both great and small. Most truthfully and lucidly has Darwin described the struggle for Existence, and named its method of action Natural Selection.

And beyond question, man, as a mere animal,

comes under the sway of these conditions; but as a human being, thoughtful and moral, he rises above the teeth-gnashing and the law of might.

Dr. Arthur Mitchell, in his recent work, on "What is Civilization?" says that "Civilization is nothing more than a complicated outcome of a war waged with Nature by man in society, to prevent her from putting into execution, in his case, her law of Natural Selection." A higher law intervenes. The moral nature can not abide the principle that "might makes right": it sees beauty in self-denial, it gains through loss and it pronounces Selfishness the crimson sin. The history of human progress will show an ever more and more successful resistance to brutal instincts; nay, this resistance *is* progress. Not, civilization produces morality; but, morality is one of the prime causes of civilization.

Hence you find morality among savages. Some instances may be of interest.

Miss Bird, in her recent work on Japan, narrates a purchase from the aborigines of that country—the Ainos—of three knives with carved handles. She offered in payment $2.50. The savages, after consultation, decided that the articles were worth only $1.10, and they would take no more.

From Henry Lansdell we learn, that the merchants of Tobolsk, Siberia, when they go north, during the summer, to purchase fish of the Samoyedes and Ostyaks, take with them flour and salt for exchange. On their return they deposit and leave unprotected at their summer stations whatever of their goods may remain unsold. Should a native pass by during the winter and need supplies of these articles, he takes what he wants, but leaves instead a notched stick as a sort of promissory note. The next season, on the return of the merchant, due payment is made in fish. So keen is the moral sense that the dealer never has cause to complain of either theft or false reckoning.

A. R. Wallace, in his "Malay Archipelago," gives a striking instance of honesty in a savage race, and under circumstances that favored dishonesty. It was in collecting birds of paradise in a small island. It was the custom of traders, at that point, to pay in advance; each native hunter agreeing to furnish birds according to the number of knives, hatchets, etc., received. On the eve of Wallace's departure, most of those who had taken prepayment, had already brought in what they had agreed to procure. One poor fellow had been so unfortunate as to secure nothing, and he had brought back the axe which had been advanced him. Another, who had agreed to bring six birds of paradise, having delivered the fifth two days before, had hurried inland for the remaining one due. This man, up to the last moment, did not return, and the boat was loaded and on the point of leaving when he came running down the beach holding up a bird, which he handed to the naturalist, saying with satisfaction, "Now I owe you nothing!"

Travellers occasionally denounce the savages among whom they move with feelings of lordly disdain, as not only immoral, but devoid of all sense of right and wrong. It must, however, be remembered how difficult it is to look at things from stand-points greatly removed from one's own; and it is well to bear in mind that few travellers understand perfectly the languages of tribes among whom they make a brief sojourn. Moreover, it is known that savages have an instinctive shrinking from stating to persons on a higher plane of thought, their dark and foolish beliefs; to say nothing of their mental incapacity to analyze and express their own emotions and abstract ideas. Trustworthy testimony of travellers and missionaries establishes the fact, that no human race exists without some, at least, feeble sense of right and wrong.

Nor, indeed, is there evidence that any such race ever existed. Recent researches into the story of prehistoric man corroborate the universal teaching of tradition and written history. The moral nature of man was back of civilization, and is underneath society and government.

And should it ever be proven that the human race were once brutal, and that ideas of right and wrong have sprung out of lower notions—as of the desirable and the dangerous—it would not at all follow, as some imagine and venture to hint, that the authority of conscience thereby is called in question, nor that the validity of moral judgments is shaken. In such a case the moral sense would still stand on the same sure foundation as Reason and Art; and the right would be just as absolutely valid as the true and the beautiful. For instance, it would make no difference with the laws of geometry, or with the facts of astronomy, that their discovery, and even that the faculty which discovered them, came, by slow evolution, from some lower form of intelligence. They are what we have found them to be. The Parthenon is no less beautiful as a temple, nor the Venus of Milo as a statue, nor the Transfiguration of Raphael as a painting, because Art was once the mere scribbling of hunting scenes upon the antler of a reindeer or the tusk of a hairy mammoth.

And morals would be quite as binding, in theory and in practice, if they could be shown to have originated, like Science and Art, from small beginnings. Things are not what they have been, if they were totally different, but what they have come to be. This is platitude, doubtless, but justified by the strange confusion existing in many able minds. Plato was once an unconscious, unborn babe; but he had become a man of sublime intelligence when he wrote the Phædrus and the Symposium. Shakespeare was once a mere infinitesimal droplet of protoplasm; but he came to be, notwithstanding this, the supreme genius of English literature. It makes no difference, then, how the moral sense arose. It exists to-day, alongside of Reason and Taste, and its judgments have a validity analogous to that of the conclusions of the exact sciences or the canons of fine art.

The important question in this connection is not, how did the moral sense arise, but what is its significance?

Surely it is fundamental in human nature, the corner-stone of civilization. So strong may it become, that it will subdue the most violent passions, deny the most eager desires, and brave torture and death. It may work without any reference to reward or punishment, here or hereafter. The most wicked of men, who neither desire nor dread a future, may have the clearest perceptions of certain kinds of duty; and very often desire to do right has brought delicate women and children deliberately to the sacrifice of all they held dear, including life itself.

A touching story, illustrating the intense vividness moral judgments may attain, and their possible elevation above all considerations of selfish desire or fear, is told of the wife of Barneveldt, the grand pensionary of Holland.

This eminent citizen of the young republic, in his old age was condemned to death for being an Arminian; and in his gray hairs was beheaded by his enemy, Prince Maurice. His heroic wife beheld her husband suffer and die in the silence of a great indignation. Two sons survived. They conspired to avenge their father by assassinating the Prince; but were detected, and one of them caught, and condemned to the scaffold. Now the proud mother interceded. Said Maurice, the Prince: "How is it that you seek pardon for your son and did not for your husband?" She replied: "My husband was innocent, but my son is guilty!" She could not beg a pardon for an innocent man—the condemned himself would have cried shame upon her; but her boy was become a manifest criminal, and could be saved not by appeal to justice, and only by suit for clemency.

Now observe, in the second place, that when

men come to act upon the notions of right or wrong, they find themselves *free* to *choose*, and the notion of personal *guilt* or *innocence* attaches not only to their doings and feelings, but to *themselves* as well. They not only see the distinction between what is right and what is wrong; but, yielding to this or to that alternative, they become sensible that they themselves deserve praise or blame. Being free to choose, they come to have *character*, good or bad, and hold themselves, and are held by others, as innocent or guilty. We are free moral agents, and hence responsible. Of this we are clearly conscious, and all our judgments of men and all self-respect and self-contempt are founded upon it.

Yet this statement needs to be carefully guarded. We are free only within very confined limits, and human accountability runs within narrow channels. When a man is brought to the judgment bar of absolute merit, many things are to be considered which the necessities of any earthly court must rule out as irrelevant.

Here is a vagabond who has committed a brutal crime. The minister of the Gospel, voicing the general sentiment of the community, and deeming the felon a responsible being, from the pulpit points a moral with the man's hardened depravity. Whereupon a physician shakes his head, and says, as the people go out of church, underbreath: "No! no! the man's brain is imperfect and his whole mental organization defective." The professional philanthropist now appears in print in a weekly religious newspaper, and writes, sorrowfully, of bad surroundings in childhood,—"the man has had no education, no occupation, and was trained in vice, and needs flowers, books and love!" A belligerent political economist responds in a secular daily that the crime was to have been expected,—"so many addled eggs in a hundred, so many vagabonds in a thousand, and such an average of suicides and murders to be expected per month!" Other correspondents cry shame upon this cold-blooded philosopher; but a man of statistics runs to his rescue, and proves that crimes come and go like storms, and are probably connected with the fluctuation of the sun-spots; and he avers that just now a criminal cyclone prevails. "Our vagabond is the victim of an epidemic, and has a touch of the murder-fever." And at last the lawyer, in his defense before the jury, pleads "moral insanity." Now all these theorists have truth in what they say, though none the whole truth.

The sphere of responsibility is circumscribed

by the conditions, good and bad, of life; and all these different advocates have just claim to patient hearing.

Pascal said that "if Cleopatra's nose had been shorter, the face of the whole world would have been changed." If the Persians had beaten the Greeks at Marathon, if Cæsar had not crossed the Rubicon, if Charles Martel had not defeated the Saracens in the battle of Tours, if Cromwell had but lived twenty years longer, if Napoleon had not made his winter campaign in Russia, how different history might have read! As nations, and even more truly as individuals, men are clearly the playthings of Destiny.

Yet, clearly the Will chooses freely within its narrow limits. It may prefer evil; it may choose good; it may act upon, or it may defy, the moral judgments of the mind.

The method of this freedom is a very great mystery. It seems to involve an act of causation, and in each determination a new beginning. It introduces into human affairs an element of caprice which, if the sphere of choice were less limited, might prove fatal to consistency, and might remove history from the domain of science.

Any one may destroy a reputation that has cost a lifetime of education, of self-repression and of active virtue, by one single deed of folly.

A touch on the trigger of a pistol pointed at a neighbor may send him to his grave, bring sorrow and want into his home, make outcasts of his children, and as well bring the doer to a prison cell and to the scaffold. The swing of Roussakof's arm, on that bloody day at St. Petersburg, killed a Czar, dissipated a national illusion, created a numerous party of revolutionists, and is now shaking to its foundations a stable and ancient despotism. Recently a capitalist of New York conveyed away five millions of dollars by a dash of his pen. A President, pondering over a bill of Congress of large financial import, by his signature changes deep channels of trade, and brings fortunes to many and ruin to thousands. More than one man in Europe could, in a day, nay, in a moment, ordain a general war, and entail upon the nations, by a mere caprice, wounds and death and impoverishment and desolation. At the battle of Trafalgar, as the British flagship, dashing into the French and Spanish fleet, silenced the *Redoubtable*, and then held her fire to receive surrender, as the smoke cleared away and revealed Nelson on the quarterdeck, glittering with the stars his heroism had won, only a touch on the trigger of a rifle in the French rigging, laid him low in his pride and robbed England of the bravest and greatest mariner that ever kinged it over the sea.

All this is passing strange, but undeniable. To will is critical. To will unwisely is fatal. It brings us to the Outermost Rim of human thought, and sets us deeply pondering what may be Beyond.

But still another important truth concerning the workings of the moral sense is to be noted. Moral action leaves the deepest impress upon the character; and long after the deed is done its results abide. If the action have been vile, there arises a persistent self-contempt and a lingering regretful memory: if it have been noble, there comes about self-respect and peaceful reminiscence.

A King Richard, crowned, amid his army and still master of his realm, must exclaim: "O coward conscience, how dost thou afflict me." But a Paul, though imprisoned and penniless and awaiting death, says calmly: "I have all and abound." "I am now ready to be offered, and the time of my departure is at hand. I have fought a good fight, I have finished my course, I have kept the faith. Henceforth, there is laid up for me a crown of righteousness, which the Lord, the righteous Judge, shall give me at that day!"

The villain may not always, like Richard the Third, come to his deserts; he may deceive his fellows or overawe the ministers of justice or buy out the law; but there sits a court within that can not so easily be cajoled nor terrified nor bribed, and he ever

> .... "Bears about
> A silent court of justice in his breast,
> Himself the judge and jury, and himself
> The prisoner at the bar, ever condemned."

Many great works of fiction have owed their power and their fascination to the sway of this law. The popular tales of all peoples, from the Greek tragedies down, have been to no small degree the illustration of the inevitable sequences of virtue and vice. Immoral novelists, at the present day, do sometimes, in defiance of their innate sense of justice, write a romance in which vice triumphs and the villain is blessed; but this simply expresses the cynicism of the narrator. Popular tales, that have voiced the common sense of the many, never have thus sinned against poetic justice.

Witness the story of the Wandering Jew; which itself has wandered over the world and finds no rest.

The narrative of the *Flying Dutchman* is also in point. A famous captain, mad to double the Cape of Storms, beaten back again and again, defied the powers of Heaven, appealed to the Devil and swore a mighty oath to persevere throughout Eternity. The Devil took him at his word. The Captain doubled the Cape, but for his impiety was doomed to roam the seas forever, from pole to pole, his phantom vessel the terror of all mariners and the dreadful herald of shipwreck.

A most interesting illustration of the sway of this law over the human imagination, appears in a passage of the "Inferno." Dante had stroked the locks of the beautiful Francesca, the daughter of his friend Guido, Lord of Ravenna; when an innocent child she had sat on his lap in the good days of old. As a woman, she had sinned; and with her betrayer she had gone to her account. And the great poet must needs meet the two in torment, still united, but now by a tie of infinite pathos in its common agony, —their punishment to be driven, driven forever of a tempest that bore them pitilessly along, on and on. One might have supposed that logic in this case would have faltered, and that loving pity had spread over, at least, his pet, the mantle of silence. But no! Dante the poet was no longer any one's advocate, and only the stern prophet of Retribution.

It will be remembered that Pontius Pilate is said to have drowned himself in the Lake of Lucerne, after, for long, hiding his shame and sorrow in the recesses of Mount Pilatus. There is a local belief, still potent in Switzerland, that a form is often seen to emerge from the water and to go through the motions of hand-washing. And, it is added, after the appearance of this awful spectre Mount Pilatus is wrapped in dark clouds, and a tempest of great fury rages.

Similar legends have everywhere abounded, revealing a deep-seated law of remorse in human nature.

But the law of conscious remorse is not all of it. Self-contempt or self-approbation work into the permanent character. The slightest actions or passions, that carry significance of right and wrong, permanently mould the character. Vice begets vulgarity, and virtue begets purity. A criminal is not only self-condemned and the upright self-approved, it is also true, as the great poet has sung—

> "He that has light within his own clear breast,
> May sit i' the center and enjoy bright day;
> But he that hides a dark soul and foul thoughts,
> Benighted walks under the midday sun:
> Himself is his own dungeon."

A Commodus, or a Cæsar Borgia, or a Marat, alongside of a St. Cæcilia, a Francis d'Assisi or a George Washington, show how low or how high human character may fall or rise. Remorse can be suppressed in time by the searing of conscience, and the peace of mind which a noble deed affords may pass away with forgetfulness of the action itself; but nothing can suppress a villainous nature nor obscure virtue. The soul is a tablet on which has been deeply engraven tokens of all deeds and feelings, good and bad; and discernment of character is the truthful reading of these fatal hieroglyphs. You are what you have made yourself to be. Circumstances condition the outer appearance of the person and the superficial display of the nature; but responsible choice carves out the permanent moral character.

To recapitulate: We have seen in the moral nature of men a sense of right and wrong, a freedom of the will enabling responsible choice, and a resulting consistent and permanent character; and we have observed that this moral nature works without any necessary relation to civil courts of justice or to personal thought of future reward and punishment.

We conclude, then, that the human conscience is as ultimate and absolute as science or art. There is a court within the breast and a code from Beyond and a sanction outside our control. And we are prepared to ask, what bearing this has upon the problem of the Ultimate Thinker and Natural Lawgiver of the Universe.

Is it not the hint of a Moral Government and of a Moral Governor, supreme over all justices and all courts?

Can the Ultimate Thinker be less than moral? If all thoughts must be first his thoughts, shall less be said of moral judgments? He, the Thinker of the True and of the Beautiful, is he not also Thinker of the Good?

And can the Natural Lawgiver be less than legislator for the human heart? Shall the Guarantee of Physics and Mechanics be less for virtue?

Man is *free*; who gave him this marvellous power? and what Divine Mystery Beyond does it reflect?

Man finds himself *responsible*, by a law within,—responsible to Whom? and in view of Whose legislation?

Men often die, perfectly aware that they have not been punished for heinous sins; nay, they may die in the commission of crime, yet the inevitable sense of guilt anticipates retribution, even when the breath is leaving the body; and the baldest materialism is ill at ease in the thought that the criminal may have escaped justice. What Tribunal Beyond, and what Judge of all the earth, shall vindicate the majesty of Right?

Surely the conscience of man is a finger pointed up to a Righteous God.

The Thinker and Natural Lawgiver of the Universe is also its Moral Governor, its Legislature, its Supreme Court and its Executive.

And Shakespeare only stated the vigorous teaching of the inmost soul, when he said—

> "In the corrupted currents of this world,
> Offence's gilded hand may show by justice;
> And oft 'tis seen, the wicked prize itself
> Buys out the law. But 'tis not so above!
> There is no shuffling, there the action lies
> In its true nature, and we ourselves compelled
> Even to the teeth and forehead of our fault,
> To give in evidence."

CHAPTER VII.

THE TEACHINGS OF MAN'S RELIGIOUS NATURE.

" If we traverse the world, it is possible to find cities without walls, without letters, without kings, without wealth, without coin, without schools, without theatres; but a city without a temple, or that practiseth not worship, prayers, and the like, no one ever saw."—PLUTARCH.

THE time has come to probe that logical necessity which has forced us to the conclusions stated in the two preceding chapters. In our study of the Physical World why were we required to infer a supreme Thinker and Lawgiver, and in our study of man's moral nature why must we accept a Judge for the soul and a Celestial Court of Last Appeal? That we were so required, no well-balanced mind can long persuade itself to deny. But why might we not have said, Nature's thoughts come without thinking, and moral judgments arise without any fixed standard of right and wrong? We could have said it, and men do occasionally say it; but Something within, deep in that Consciousness which lies back of all knowledge, would have laughed the foolish words to scorn.

There are some things the mind, by its ultimate structure, requires us to believe. They may be verbally denied, but the denial only argues that the objector is either mentally immature or mentally lacking. Of these, Personal Existence is one. You can not prove that you exist, and some crazed philosophers have denied or questioned it; but every man believes it, notwithstanding, and it is taken for granted in every word uttered, emotion felt or deed done. Personal Identity is another of these fundamental postulates of human intelligence. It can be proved only by reference to the substructure of the human mind. You are conscious that you are, and have remained, yourself; and this is all the account you can give of the matter. Should any acquaintance claim to have become some one else, should any public character declare himself another,—should, for instance, Hayes appear at the White House and demand recognition as President Garfield,— pity would be uppermost, and a lunatic asylum suggest itself as a fitting remedy for such madness.

We can not think, except under limitations of *Time* and *Space;* but try to prove that these ideas have objective validity, and any argument that can be framed, except appeal to mental necessity, must be insufficient.

There is thus a substructure to human reason, undeniable, unquestionable and unprovable, a faculty of faith in ultimate things which furnishes laws to regulate thought.

Now, it is in this substructure of human intelligence that the necessity for inferences from Nature to a Deity lies.

For here, among ultimate things, is a clear faith in the Absolute, in a Something unconditioned by time, space or aught that doth the universe inhabit.

This Absolute is not a mere idea—no empty category of thought, any more than is Personal Existence and Identity, or Time and Space; it is an intuition of Being. This is what makes it a regulative law of thinking. If it be not valid, then is nothing valid,—

> "The pillared firmament is rottenness,
> And earth's base built on stubble."

Thinking requires, as one of its conditions, that we shall assume, back of the finite, an Infinite, and back of the conditioned, an Absolute. The Absolute is a sort of Firmament in thought, a majestic Overhead and Background for any philosophy. It can not be gotten rid of, any more than landscape can avoid its sky. Indefinitely extended space does not cover the notion of Infinity, and indefinitely prolonged time does not make out Eternity. Infinity and Eternity are incomposite and indivisible. Only the Absolute is Infinite and Eternal. The human mind postulates an Unconditioned Condition of all things, an Uncaused Cause of all things. And who else may be the Ultimate Thinker and Lawgiver of Nature and the Supreme Court of the Soul but This? This is God.

And hence atheism never makes lasting progress, any more than do other fantastic and unnatural schemes of philosophy. This or that dull savage may ignore, or this or that crackbrained sage deny, a Deity; but directly the human mind comes true again to its intuition, and the folly does not spread. Indeed atheism, when sincere, is a form of idiocy. The atheist is mentally lacking. He may, in other regards, be a great genius; but in this concern his mind is undeveloped, or perhaps totally at fault. As men are born lacking in mental or moral sense, so doubtless some fail of a religious nature. This proves only what may otherwise be learned in idiot asylums and State prisons: that the laws of inheritance at times work at cross purposes and produce but sorry results.

But suppose some should argue, with reference to this mental necessity (as we saw in the last chapter, some have argued with reference to the moral necessities of our natures)—suppose some should insist that man was once an ape, and that the belief in a God has grown up through lower forms of thought and is but a product of inherited brain structure modified by evolution, and hence of no real validity.

We should reply, as in the matter of growth in moral ideas—for the problem is substantially the same—that there is no evidence of our race ever having been brutal, and that even granting this were so, the law of consciousness, though recently evolved, would still be valid, just as are laws of mathematics, of physics and of art, though recently perceived. Religion is just as little called in question, by its small beginnings, as art or science. You do not gauge Plato or Shakespeare at time of birth, but in their maturity. What the human mind was before it matured, is of as little interest to us, in this connection, as what Plato might have been ere he was born, or Shakespeare ere he learned to talk.

The human mind is what it has come to be; and as a regulator of thought, is most valuable to us in its most perfect development.

That men were at first children, and that many men are now childish, must be granted. That the great masses of mankind never once in their lives think upon the Absolute, is undeniable. This intuition of the Absolute belongs to the foundation, and hence is under ground and hidden out of sight, unless one descend into the depths of the mind; but none the less upon it rests the whole structure of thought. It is a mystery, as much so, and more so even, than Personal Existence or Identity, than Space or Time. It furnishes the rational explanation and justification of the world's religious history. Its consideration is for philosophers.

Men believed in a Deity long before they argued the matter out; and they do not now believe because they argue it out. They accept of a mental necessity, which is in general not clearly recognized. Just as men talked before they understood the laws of language; and do not now converse because they have studied grammar. Just as men walked before they had studied anatomy; and walk now without any reference to anatomy. The logical basis of religion is one thing, its history quite another.

It makes no difference, then, how the religious nature historically arose—any more than how Art, Science and Morals arose. It exists, a magnificent edifice, built upon solid rock. Its validity is precisely as unimpeachable as that of any other department of human intelligence; and the all-important question is not as to how religion developed, but as to its significance, and how one may so obey the divine impulse in his breast as to honor his own higher nature and best fulfil his destiny.

Nor does it at all affect the truth of this position, that men, left to their natural instincts, have in general ignored the Absolute Deity and bowed down to many petty divinities, and even to idols manufactured by their own hands. This was simply a faulty working of human intelligence, analogous to the general feebleness of popular conceptions on any profound subject of reflection. It does not invalidate the claims of the religious nature; any more than the fact that savages can not multiply or divide, invalidates the theorems of Euclid or the Principia of Newton. Whenever in history the human mind has matured to its manhood, not only have mathematical and other scientific laws asserted themselves effectively, the religious nature of man has ever risen to contemplation of the Absolute God, and Mythology has been to far-seeing eyes but the transparent veil hung by human childishness before the Awful Glory of Deity. The Egyptians, amid their gross idolatry, well knew the One God and Father of All. In Greece and in India the Deity was the Background to all earnest thinking. Socrates argued for a creative God almost as forcibly as Paley. .

But after we have answered all the atheistical objections, there still remains the Epicurean cry of "Cui bono?" "Of what benefit is theology? What practical knowledge can we have of this Divine Firmament of thought, this majestic but indistinct Background of the Absolute! Our very thinking of Him, conditions Him and degrades Him from His godhood. To know Him is to be ignorant of Him." But would not such an argument prove as well that the little child can not know its own father? We all are, indeed, only creeping babes in theology. Our loftiest conceptions of God and of His powers are but childish gropings. We can at best understand His ways only after the inattentive, feeble and puzzled way of infancy. The completest descriptions we can give of His attributes must fail to express His fulness. But is it not knowledge? It surely is not comprehension; it is merest apprehension, and that of a babe. But it is sufficient to enable the child to recognize the Father.

Natural Theology is not at all a region of exact knowledge, and we can not expect clear outlines: it is the sphere of intuition, of aspiration and of devotion. An idea of God that were perfectly comprehensible we could reject at once, as palpably false; just as any conception of the Universe, which left nothing to be explained, would thereby show itself a silly lie. We must be content to admit, with Augustine, that "God is greater and truer in our thoughts than in our words: He is greater and truer in reality than in our thoughts!" We each have our horizon. Men may rise in altitude and the horizon may ever widen; but no mere man can reach limitless vision. Nor may angels, archangels, nor heavenly principalities. The highest celestial being has his horizon. God only beholds no limit to His view and brooks no restraint upon His powers.

We claim, then, as the first teaching of the religious nature of man, that there is a God.

Its second teaching is a bidding to *worship*.

Here again we are pointed down to the substructure of the mind,—this time, however, to the foundation of the Emotional rather than of the Rational department of Intelligence.

To worship God is as much an instinct, as to believe in God is an intuition. It is a religious soul-necessity.

Not but that men may ignore it—as the necessity is moral,—not but that they may respond imperfectly. It is simply a *spiritual pressure* within; and men yield to it, in a thousand different degrees and with a thousand differing forms, according to the depth of their natures, their educations and their surroundings.

Nor does it concern us to ask how worship arose, nor through what brutalities it progressed; ere Moses bowed at the Burning Bush, ere Christ enjoined upon the Samaritan Woman at Jacob's Well the spiritual worship of a Spiritual Deity, ere Paul on Mars' Hill pointed the idolaters of Athens to the Unknown God, "in whom we live and move and have our being."

And if any complain that it is impossible to decide, from the light of Nature, whom to worship, or when or how or where, this does not prove darkness, but only dimness; and it is no stretch of probability to surmise that whosoever approaches Deity according to his light, such as it is, will surely not fail of divine recognition, be the time, place or form what it may.

If reasons are demanded, we can give many why the creature should recognize the Creator, why the finite should rest upon the Arm of the Infinite, why the puzzled human mind should commune with the Thinker of all thoughts; but these arguments will each only bring us to a fundamental oughtness. God is because He is; and He ought to be worshipped because He ought to be worshipped. Necessity is laid upon us in and by the constitution of things. We are made to reflect and glorify, to study, admire, praise, thank and obey Him. The man who questions it is like the child that challenges the obligation to respect and love its father. Well said Epictetus: "If I were a nightingale, I would act the part of a nightingale,—if a swan, the part of a swan; but since I am a reasonable creature, it is my duty to praise God."

Again, the religious nature teaches us of a divine *Providence*, and most naturally we *pray*. This is an inevitable inference from what has gone on before, here and in the preceding chapters. The Creator, Preserver and Aim of the Universe,—the Thinker and Lawgiver of Nature,—the Moral Governor and Supreme Court of the Soul,—the Deity whom we perforce recognize by intuition and worship by instinct, it is inconceivable that He should be improvident of us or unjust toward us, in any of His dealings. Many things happening that look to the contrary conclusion, can not shake this faith. The cloud that rests over the world does not shadow God.

And so Socrates could say to his judges, himself expecting death: "Wherefore, O judges, be of good cheer about death, and know this of a truth: that no evil can happen to a good man either in life or after death." And Plato further could urge: "Then this must be our notion of the just man; that even when he is in poverty or sickness or any other seeming misfortune, all things will in the end work together for good to him in life and death, for the gods have a care of any one whose desire is to be just and to be like God, as far as man can attain His likeness by the pursuit of virtue."

Ages before Christ, and probably even before Moses, the Deity was spoken of in Egypt, by the initiated, as "Father." He was described in such words as "Rock of Truth is thy Name"; "He wipes tears from off all faces"; "Every one glorifies thy goodness; mild is thy love toward us; thy tenderness surrounds our hearts; great is thy love in all the souls of men." The human mind, in its maturity, always has recognized the essential goodness of God.

And appeal to that Goodness in *prayer* always has been found consistent with the highest philosophy. Cleanthes, Euripides, Socrates, Epictetus, Marcus Antoninus and many other sages of antiquity, all have left behind them, though guided only by the light of Nature, beautiful and earnest prayers. Take these, for instance: Socrates, in Phædrus, prayed, "Grant me to become beautiful in the inner man, and that, whatever outward things I have, may be at peace with those within. May I deem the wise man rich, and may I have such a portion of gold as none but a prudent man can either bear or employ." In Euripides we have the prayer, "Thou God of all, infuse light into the souls of men, whereby they may be enabled to know what is the root from whence all their evils spring, and by what means they may avoid them."

Still another teaching of the religious nature is *Immortality*. Here again we have an inference, and urged on by a mighty yearning.

Immortality is something quite different from that mere love of life and shrinking from death which man shares with the brute.

A belief in it appeared in very early times, and expressed the ambition of wise and good men. It became the teaching of philosophies, which have swayed the thinking world in all succeeding ages. Cicero wrote this sentence from amid a generation of gross sensualists and a coterie of literary believers in annihilation: "There is, I know not how, in minds, a certain presage of a future existence; and this takes the deepest root, and is the most discoverable, in the greatest geniuses and most exalted souls." At first, this presage was matter of speculation; but in time it descended from its hints in Orphic hymns, its hidden teachings in Eleusinian mysteries, and its fine-spun academic subtleties, into the daily life of men. Immortality became a Hope; and it was a blessed hope already, when Revelation made it a Certainty.

Many arguments to prove the Immortality of the Soul have been ventured by spiritual minds; but they have served, like syllogistic arguments for the being and the worship of a God, to bring out the spiritual necessities of religious thought and experience rather than to prove an incontestable conclusion.

It may be profitable briefly to review some of these. Thus, a future life is needed to explain this. It seems irrational, that the mind should be challenged to the study of life and of death, of time and of eternity, of the Universe and of God, only to be mocked by its incapacity. There is a sharp incongruity in the creation of an intelligence made only for failure. It is intolerable to think, that the problems that have puzzled us, here below, are not for us to be solved, somewhere and at some time.

But not only thought is interrupted by death, virtue is left unfinished. Man is capable of most wonderful expansion of moral powers. He grows in grace, yet ever the law of virtue remains for him an ideal. His whole being fills with a desire to attain; yet ever he fails of perfection. Death sharply interrupts the process. Yet the imagination prolongs it, can not but prolong it, into another existence. It seems extremely improbable, that what was the highest aim of life below, should be miserably balked, and by the wise and upright Judge, just short of attainment. Unless human life be aimless, and human virtue a mere shadow and vanity of vanities, all vanity! this earthly walk is a sojourn, and Home Beyond.

Moreover, the sense of justice, fully treated in the preceding chapter, demands a future existence for reward and punishment. To aver that the wicked suffer and that the good prosper, according to their several merits, is to assert what manifestly fails to take place. The moral government of this world, as regards individuals, is as unfinished and unsatisfactory as human philosophy or human virtue. And, moreover, after the fullest vindication of human law, the moral sense, as regards any criminal, still remains disturbed. There ought to be a future to right wrongs, to punish guilt and to reward virtue.

These arguments not only carry such conviction as may be in them; they surely reveal a deep-seated tendency in human nature to look Beyond; and they explain that mighty yearning for eternal life, which had already taken a deep hold of many religious natures when Jesus came to bring life and immortality to light, through the Gospel.

CHAPTER VIII.

GOD IN HISTORY.

"*Behind the suns, rest suns in the farthest sky. Their distant ray, these thousands of years, has been flying toward the tiny earth and has reached it not.*

"*O Thou tender, near God! Scarcely does the human spirit open its little babe's eye, ere Thou beamest in upon it, O Sun of the suns and of spirits!*"—RICHTER.

VOICES from Beyond are clearly heard in human *history*. As in certain very interesting laws that suggest, with irresistible persuasiveness, a Divine Presence in human affairs, and that find no explanation on any atheistic or agnostic hypothesis. To these attention is called.

And first, to the great pictorial law of *Retributive Justice*. There works in history a majestic system of moral compensations that quite lie beyond the sphere of personal guilt and innocence. History is eminently a moral drama and a kind of poetic justice, treating nations, races and communities as though they were responsible individuals, and ages as though only a lifetime, deals out general reward and punishment. The sins and the virtues of the fathers are visited upon the children. The process may be a long one, but it is effective. An inevitable succession of moral cause and effect in history, runs parallel to the inevitable sequence of natural cause and effect in the physical world. The Greeks had a proverb which expressed sense of this justice of Destiny: "The mills of the gods grind slow, but they grind fine." The themes of the famous Greek drama derived interest largely from this firm belief in a divine Nemesis. All history owes to this somewhat of its fascination.

With extreme cases of pictorial retribution all are familiar. Marius at Carthage, Cæsar at the statue of Pompey, Napoleon at St. Helena, and a thousand similar vivid pictures, point a moral not only on the fickleness of fortune, but still more on the irony of justice. Every one from childhood has heard of empires weighed in the balance and found wanting, doomed to overthrow, and long since become but a memory. In all the great historic centers of ancient times are ruins of silent cities, grim tokens not only of the mortality of man, but as well of the frailty of civilizations. As the traveller stands on the pyramid or paces the deserted thoroughfares of the disentombed city, he is reminded not only of the genius and energy which erected these monuments, and of the beauty, wealth and wit that once adorned these habitations, but not less of the completeness of the overthrow. He is tempted to sigh with the Hebrew prophet, in contemplation of the overthrow of Babylon, "How hast thou fallen, O day-star, son of the morning?" He reflects upon the degeneracy which provoked the ruin. The lesson finds utterance in few words,—great gifts misused, morality defied, justice forgotten, and therefore disaster creeping in, and final and utter collapse.

Indeed, the law of retribution is fully exposited only in the history of a great nation. Men, as individuals, die, so soon as their native stock of vitality is exhausted, regardless of their virtues; and they may perish while yet they prosper in their sins. But communities and races and nations live on and on; and moral causes, in these cases, have time to bring about appropriate effects.

There is no reason why nations should die a natural death. National death is always unnatural. So far from its being true that nations die out of themselves in time, as some claim, it is rather undeniable that there is in mankind a recuperative energy. As the Hebrews were wont to put it: the sins of the fathers are visited upon the children to the third and fourth generations, but their virtues descend unto thousands of generations. In other words, the evil tendencies of human nature are of themselves short-lived and prone to work out, while the good energies of mankind indefinitely persist and multiply. Races ought thus, though getting their deserts in sorrow and disaster by the way, on the whole, to rise in power and to increase in vigor; while the individual grows old and dies, the race ought to be immortal, and renew its youth from age to age.

Where a race decays, where a national life collapses, there must have been unusual squandering of advantages and gross betrayal of trusts.

But the forgotten mounds and the silent cities emphasize only extreme instances of the working of the law. It is powerful and active with all races however progressive, and all ages however free from decay. "The fathers eat sour grapes, and the children's teeth are set on edge": one generation sins, and the next suffers. Cromwell slaughtered Irishmen, seized their lands, and imposed unjust laws; and all generations of Englishmen since have been disturbed by the furious hatred of their victims, and will be forever until the wrong is righted and the expiation wrought out.

Our American ancestors imported negroes to

work on the Southern plantations, and we of to-day must endure and, with blood and tears, abate the evils of slavery. This law of retribution gives sublimity to history, and largely furnishes the fascination of historic research.

But it will be urged that this is not strictly retribution. It would not be just to punish one generation for what another has done. It is poetic justice. It is only *pictorial retribution.* It is a sublime picture-lesson, illustrating the logic of personal desert. In the history of a community or nation we see fully portrayed that moral persistency of cause and effect which, in the individual life, is rudely cut asunder by death.

Peoples sin and suffer, and perhaps perish; and men are warned against that degeneracy which shall, in every vicious life, inevitably provoke punishment and result in ruin.

But *whose* parable is this pictorial illumination of human history in the interest of morals and of religion? Is it not the Voice of God using events for words? Is it not God in history?

A second indication of God in history may be had in the law of *sacrifice.* This is what furnishes the *heroic* element in human affairs. Men are not only animals to fight and hate and struggle for existence, an inner spiritual possibility renders them a little lower than the angels. Men are capable of self-denial. As animals in Nature, they may, and must, struggle to earn daily bread in competition with one another; but as intelligent beings in history they are bound to humanity and charity. Herein we are distinguished from the merely physical world; and yet it ought to be remarked, in passing, that at least a *foreshadowing* of the law of sacrifice is found in the physical world. There is an involuntary sacrifice to which all things are subject. Every animate or inanimate object has an end beyond itself, for the attainment of which it is liable at any time to be offered up. If plants are to grow, the soil must yield its richest juices and minerals: if animals are to survive, many plants must surrender foliage and fruit: if man is to prosper, cattle must labor, suffer and be slaughtered. If truths are to prevail, if reforms are to be carried out, if government is to be maintained or society preserved, many men and women must involuntarily lose happiness, limbs, and it may be life, that their "dead selves" may become "stepping-stones to higher things." Every means looks toward an end, and every end, sooner or later, to greater or less degree, must yield its own objective importance for the furtherance of ends still beyond.

Look at these delicate seedlings that press up into the May sunshine. They are called annuals; but pluck the blossom in the bud and they will live *two* seasons. The work of perfecting seed shortens their career. Leave them to themselves and they will blossom and die. They die that their offspring may live.

The lioness will protect her whelp till she lies stretched at its side in willing death. The pelican will give her blood to the thirsting chicks. Darwin tells of an ape, that rescued a wounded comrade from within the range of a dozen flashing rifles, to carry his brother brute dauntlessly up the mountain-side. Warrior ants will fight for their community with a desperate devotion of limb and life, which the fiercest human fanatic or the most thoroughly seasoned human veteran never attains. Many a man's life has been saved by a dog or a horse, at cost of self-destruction.

It will be noticed that all this is *involuntary* and *pictorial*. The law of Sacrifice in Nature, like the law of Retribution in History, is a poetic foreshadowing of sublimities of character and great concerns of destiny. It is Nature's prophecy of virtue, which she utters in the lower to realize in the higher world.

The *voluntary* and *noble* sacrifice observable in history commences in childhood; and as life advances, ever more emphatically does it become, for every human being, the obligation, and, indeed, the gauge of virtue. A father's or a mother's love, what endless self-denials does it necessitate! The family is preserved and the home made happy only by the voluntary unselfishness of all its inmates. In civil relations, how much property, time and often blood, in taxes and in service, must be devoted, in order to insure the public weal. During our late civil war, the North alone gave to death 300,000 of her bravest youth and expended four billions of her wealth, for the integrity of the Union.

Consider an event like the following; and it stands not alone in the story of human strifes.

At a now long-since-forgotten battle of the Middle Ages (of St. Jacob, in 1600), a body of Swiss mountaineers, amid their own hills, fought a far superior army, composed of the *élite* of French chivalry. The contest was utterly unequal. The French knights and men-at-arms were clad in superior armor, warriors from their youth and trained to military manœuvres and achievement; while the Swiss peasants had only rude weapons, scanty armor and no discipline. But to submit was shameful. To save their liberties they must conquer. So they battled with quenchless ardor and sublime courage;

and death seemed as nothing at all, compared with slavery. Not one fled; and there they died, falling like the Spartans of old at Thermopylæ,—died to a man, amid heaps of smitten foes.

Or take a still more striking instance of unselfish heroism, more striking because deliberate and in no wise influenced by the mere momentary battle-glow of physical courage.

A race of men, who for ages had battled with the sea, shutting out the ocean from its salt meadows to replace waves with orchards, gardens, factories and cities, were striving, in dire earnestness, to force back such a tide of tyranny and bloodthirsty cruelty as seldom has threatened to engulf any civilization. William the Silent, Prince of Orange, the unchallenged peer of Washington, had been assassinated by a Spanish emissary, and Maurice, his son, destined to become the greatest general and statesman of his age, was hardly more than a youth; but the persistency of the heroic Dutch was beginning to tell upon the resources of their oppressors. The ships of the States were beginning to sweep the seas of Spanish treasure; and their soldiers were becoming apt to war and a fair match for the terrible Spanish infantry.

It was Saturday evening, in an ancient town

on a canal, a fortified place, garrisoned by the mercenaries of Spain. The winter had been long and cold, and fuel was become scarce. A boat, loaded with turf, had just come through the water-gate. Some Italian hirelings had hurried on board to get the needed supplies, and then had dragged the vessel near the guard-house. A crowd of soldiers tramped over the deck, and an officer lounged for a while in the cabin. A servant of some high official complained of the turf, "his master would never be satisfied with its inferior quality." "Oh!" remarked the skipper, "the best part of the cargo is underneath, kept expressly for the Captain: he will be sure to get enough of it to-morrow."

But hark! what was that?—a cough?—a sneeze? down in the hold? Every one would have said so, had not the pumps made such a racket. A leak, it seems, had been sprung in coming up the canal; and the skipper and his brother were working the pumps as if cargo and life depended upon it; and in their excitement were bawling to one another the simplest directions in voice of thunder. If a hundred men had sneezed down below, no one could have detected them in such uproar. Surely never were noisier seamen on a Dutch canal.

And now night is come, darkness is fallen, the crowd is gone, the guard are asleep, the city in repose, the skipper and his brother alone. See them creep into the little cabin and anxiously open a trap-door in the floor and peer into the cold, damp gloom of the hold. "Come forth, good fellows, the way is clear!" What are these?—seventy armed men, packed together like sardines, up to their knees in icy-cold water, cramped with the chill, nigh suffocated of foul air and faint with hunger and thirst. From Monday until Saturday night, with only one brief release, they have thus sat, while the boat has encountered contrary winds and blocks of ice. Surely one might say, "Patients for the hospital." But no, rather heroes girded up for battle and for victory, they shall warm themselves with deadly blows and quench their thirst in red blood. Yonder lieutenant, while the soldiers of Spain were tramping the deck, overcome of cold and dampness, began to sneeze. Drawing his dagger, he besought his next comrade to stab him to the heart lest he betray them to their foe. That man's name was Held, which being interpreted means "hero"!

It is scarce necessary to pause upon the sequel. Seventy such heroes, armed and in the streets of a small sleeping city, would find it easy to slaughter the guard, to open the gates and to let Prince Maurice in. Thus began a series of victories that ended in the destruction of Spanish prestige, the establishment of national independence and a consequent commercial prosperity, up to that time unsurpassed in the world's history.

Those seventy heroes were rough soldiers, very likely rendered bloodthirsty by years of conflict with a foe that knew no mercy. It is doubtful whether they went to church very often, prayed much or gave alms to the poor. They drank enormous quantities of beer and worse liquors, were profane and in many cases licentious. Yet all hardships they suffered for liberty: all perils they ventured for the deliverance of their country. They freely offered themselves as sacrifices for the State. They stood between their homes and a licentious foreign soldiery, between their churches and the Inquisition, between their council-halls and a foreign tyranny.

But why should they have done so, and why do we praise them for thus ignoring their personal risk and acting in heroic self-denial?

And this is only one incident, in history, of sublime heroism: they are numberless. Indeed, the narrative would have had no right to a place in this work had it not been typical. The story is a parable. It reveals a law. History details a thousand such and with the same lesson. But notice how seemingly unreasonable this law is, at least from the natural stand-point. It certainly appears, on the face of it, irrational and much more unfair, that one man must suffer in behalf of another, as the cost of virtue. Yet all the world applauds this self-devotion. We shake our heads over it in perplexity; but our hearts leap for joy, and our proudest claim for man is that he is capable of this heroic self-forgetfulness.

So all-compelling is this law of sacrifice that it finds its way into religions, and becomes inevitably a part of every scheme of worship. It may be an offering of first-fruits or a shedding of the blood of rams or of bullocks. It may be a sacrifice of the fairest of the captives. It may be a sprinkling of human blood upon an idol. A father burns his dearest child on the brazen knees of Moloch, or a mother throws her babe into the Ganges to crocodiles. The devotee perhaps submits his own members to torture, and swings on an iron hook or lies down on a bed of spikes or lives year by year tormented by sackcloth and flagellations and fastings and vigils.

Dr. Rein, in his recent work of "Travels in Japan," recounts a popular legend, significant of the beliefs of the common people, a sad legend of a gentle wife, who, knowing her husband's ship to be out upon the deep in a wild storm, herself sprang into the raging sea to propitiate the angry gods, and so secure, at expense of her own faithful life, the safety of her beloved.

At times worship has assumed the form of a stately ritual of horrors: priests have been made murderers by profession, and the taking of life considered the most acceptable homage of the religious nature to Deity. The Aztec civilization of Mexico yearly sacrificed thousands of victims. On one red year over one hundred thousand wretches died in honor of the gods. Multitudes stood breathless and adoring about the pyramid temples, as the captives were taken to the summit, and there, in view of all, were slain, the chief priest tearing out the still quivering heart to hold it up an offering to the Sun.

One of the customs of the Aztecs was very remarkable. A beautiful captive was annually sacrificed to Tezcatlipoca. For a whole year he was treated and worshipped as a god. He was attended by pages and thronged by a prostrating multitude, whithersoever he was led. On the fatal day a solemn procession followed him to the temple, and there he was offered up as an impersonation of a good divinity, with elaborately respectful and devout ceremonies.

But what can be more manifest than the logical absurdity of this rite of sacrifice? The fruits and flowers are clearly of no use to Deity; and the shedding of blood is brutal, even when only animals are the victims. How can Deity be pleased with waste? how much less with murder? Do we not, in all this groping of the natural man, but discern the human mind, led by a divine instinct, approaching blindly the great truth that the highest act of worship is self-sacrifice, and the noblest form of virtue unselfishness?

Indeed sacrifice, whether as a law of conduct or as a rite, is an instinct perplexed, that gropes toward the light through a dismal labyrinth of errors. It tends to urge mankind up toward the Golden Rule of virtue. As Justice in history is pictorial of that Divine Judgment Bar before which the soul, in its guilt or in its innocence, is arraigned: so Sacrifice is pictorial of that perfect virtue which fulfils law. And if we call the Vengeance that overtakes vice and crime, in the course of history, Pictorial Retribution, we must as well name Sacrifice, *Pictorial Virtue.*

But Whose picture? and why in the interest of Morals and Religion? Is it not again the Voice of God, using facts for words? Is it not God in History?

Once more,—the presence of God in human events is indicated by the law of *sorrow*. And this is what gives *pathos* to history. There is an enlightening and purifying mission of adversity. Trouble, borne in the right spirit, opens the eyes and improves the character. As Alfred de Musset, speaking out of bitter experience, has told us, "No one knows himself, until he has suffered." The merchant succeeds often because once he failed. The philosopher suffers nothing from a rebuff to his conceit. The author does better by the world, that his first book in vain sought a publisher. The king, dethroned and exiled, is often a far nobler man than the monarch glittering in his crown and sceptre amid flatterers.

It can not be said that this law of sorrow disposes of the awful problem of evil in the world; and still less may it be denied that pains anger and harden rebellious natures. But it remains true, after all that has been said by the cynic, that there is a use in dark things, and that grief may be allowed by the willing disposition to mellow and sweeten and beautify the soul. Diderot declared, " Prosperity unmasks the vices: adversity reveals the virtues." He might have also averred,—for it is true,— that prosperity provokes the vices and that adversity begets the virtues. The world is the better that a shadow rests upon it. Dr. Bushnell, after the death of his only child, said: "I have learned more of experimental religion since my little boy died than in all my life before." As an English poet has lately sung:

"Were there no night, we could not read the stars,
    The heavens would turn into a blinding glare:
Freedom is best seen through the prison bars,
    And rough seas make the haven passing fair.

"We can not measure joys but by their loss:
    When blessings fade away we see them then:
Our richest clusters grow around the Cross;
    And in the night-time angels sing to men.

"The seed must first lie buried deep in earth,
    Before the lily opens to the sky;
So 'light is sown,' and gladness has its birth,
    In the dark deeps where we can only cry.

"Life out of death, is Heaven's unwritten law,
    Nay, it is written in a myriad forms;
The victor's palm grows on the field of war,
    And strength and beauty are the fruit of storms."

But consider what this means. Is it not also, like the laws of Retribution and of Sacrifice, a pressure toward development of character and in the interest of the largest concerns of human destiny? If through humbling at God's hand man is exalted, not only is sorrow justified and explained: shall not also *humility* appear as the fitting attitude of the soul before the Almighty? Nay, if the law of Justice in history be Pictorial Retribution and the law of Sacrifice Pictorial Virtue, then is this law of Sorrow *Pictorial Humility*.

But Whose picture? and why in the interests of Morals and Religion? Is it not, still again, the Voice of God using experiences the tenderest and deepest for words, words of O so great import? Is it not God in History?

Well sang a gentle nature, upon whom grief had wrought a lovely work of grace:

> "There is no God, the foolish saith,
>   But none, there is no sorrow;
> And Nature oft the cry of faith
>   In bitter need will borrow.
> Eyes, which the preacher could not school,
>   By wayside graves are raised;
> And lips say, 'God be pitiful!'
>   That ne'er said, 'God be praised!'"

Attention has now been directed to three great laws that ever work in history, and which no agnostic nor atheistic hypothesis can at all account for nor in any wise explain,—the laws of Justice or Pictorial Retribution, of Sacrifice or Pictorial Virtue and of Sorrow or Pictorial Humility. These three great principles lend to the story of human events its fascination.

They lift history above the pettiness of men's foibles, and render it tragic, heroic and pathetic. But they do much more. They are each voices of God, uttering in events, in facts and in experiences, parables of God's attitude toward men and of what ought to be man's attitude toward God.

PART III.

THE MYSTERY OF GODLINESS.

CHAPTER IX.

INSPIRED GENIUS.

> .... "*Heaven-taught lyre*
> *None but the noblest passions to inspire.*"
> —LYTTLETON.

WE have now proceeded far enough in our meditations upon the mysteries of life to find ourselves perforce querying: whether human genius ever becomes so far supernatural as to recognize by a divine insight, and declare by an authoritative revelation, truths from Beyond, unperceived of the ordinary eye and unprovided for in the common organization of human intelligence.

Is Nature our only guide in morals and religion, and her Dimness our only light? Have we but hints, intuitions, instincts and inferences?

Surely there is no inherent improbability in

the rise, from time to time, of men gifted with inspired genius. One might naturally expect history to produce occasionally luminous souls that should enlighten the comparative darkness of Nature. It is quite rational to surmise the existence of some provision for the religious growth of mankind.

This never has seemed improbable to any race or class of men.

Prophecy founds itself substantially upon human needs. It is hard to worship a Being who remains eternally silent; and in no way can the Divine Thinker and Lawgiver communicate with His creatures more directly or effectively than by the illumination of some mediating mind. Hence the idea of inspiration of some sort comes naturally and with show of reason to all religious natures, in all ages and in every clime. If real illumination fail, clairvoyance or fraud must take its place. The prophet, let him be called nabi, vates, mantis, druid, dervish or medicine-man, will ever be found speaking authoritatively on divine things.

This need, and its universal recognition, are of profound significance to the thoughtful. The reverent student of religions will not despise these many jarring voices, but rather will seek patiently to learn of what Substance these insubstantialities are the shadows. Doubtless these superstitions are mirage; but let us remember that mirage is, after all, the unusual refraction of a real, far-away landscape.

We have found that in human history all the higher laws of knowledge, taste and emotion work progressively. The beginnings of the various arts and sciences have ever been rude; but they foreshadowed coming sublimities of the Beautiful and the True. In like manner the law of prophecy ought to elucidate and justify itself. History may reasonably be expected, in some of its chapters, to give us a genuine inspiration authoritative and convincing, as she has given us science and art in glorious maturity.

Nor has there been any failure in this regard. Prophecy has as truly risen above its small beginnings as any art or science, and as veritably become a channel for human genius as painting, sculpture, mathematics or chemistry.

It will be the purpose of this chapter to fix the reader's attention upon the most remarkable series of phenomena, of the sort we are contemplating, the world has as yet produced—an outburst of religious feeling perfectly unique, complete in itself, and not less than sublime.

It is evident that we may wisely and fairly ignore all feebler manifestations. For if there be a higher supernatural law guaranteeing the possibility of a divine inspiration of certain prophetic natures, we may be sure it will best verify and explain itself in its most luminous workings. We do not go to savages to learn the largest forthcome of the moral nature, but to philanthropists like Gautama, Confucius and Christ. We do not ask of the brutal and superstitious instruction in natural theology: we sit down rather at the feet of men of religious insight, like Moses, Pythagoras and Christ. All arts and all sciences have their masters, in whom the law of their craft is potent, and whose voices only are authoritative. The study of the wild and fitful workings of the prophetic fervor in savage, barbarous and idolatrous races serves simply as encouragement for us to seek, with hopeful heart, that grandest outburst of religious feeling history records—Hebrew Prophecy. A candid study of the facts involved in the story of the Hebrew prophets will fall little short of converting a general sense of the need and probability of divine inspiration into an assurance.

Here were a class of men, and their history extending over many centuries, of intense individuality, who yet believed themselves to be under the sway of the Divine Spirit. Simple-hearted, unselfish, conscientious, devoted, they spoke for God. Imposture, in most cases at least, was wholly out of the question. They were, as a class, able, honorable and in earnest unto death.

The Greek word προφήτης gives the best idea of the work they claimed to do. The preposition in this noun indicates not precedence, but mediation. The prophet spake *for* God. This is the strictly classical usage of the term. Apollo is called by Æschylus the προφήτης of Zeus, the Pithia by Herodotus the προφῆτις of Apollo. And the term is very properly employed in the New Testament to express the simple hortatory utterance of truth, a meaning which, in English, the word prophecy has only recently lost. That the Greek term was well chosen by the Seventy to translate the Hebrew name "nabi," is apparent from a few words in Exodus. "The Lord said unto Moses, 'I have made thee a God to Pharaoh, and Aaron thy brother shall be thy nabi'"; which explains itself fully in a preceding paragraph: "'he shall be thy spokesman unto the people: and he shall be, even he shall be to thee instead of a mouth, and thou shalt be to him instead of God.'" The Hebrew nabi was the divine *mouthpiece*. The utterance of the Divine Counsel, by word and by symbol, was his appropriate sphere of action.

And this was never forgotten. The Hebrew

prophets were the guardians of literature: music and song formed part of their collegiate education, and the writings of many of them give evidence of careful training in composition and rhetoric; but they never lost view of the fact that they were only Voices. Personality in authorship and notions of copyright were entirely foreign to their habits of thought. What they spake was the "Word of the Lord"; and it belonged to the people of God.

They were annalists, and the greater portion of the historical parts of the Old Testament came from their reeds, and much that they wrote is lost; but their spirit was neither scientific nor literary, and their object was mainly to illuminate and apply to history their theology and ethics.

At times they forecast the future. Elijah foretold the famine. Jeremiah prophesied the death of Hananiah. Isaiah accurately described beforehand the downfall of Babylon and Tyre. But even this was incidental. The prophets were not chiefly diviners; and there could be no greater mistake than to suppose that this gift of prediction ever degenerated into mere fortune-telling.

The prophet's foreknowledge, like his music, his poetry and his history, was but a kind of voice to utter the Word of the Lord.

Pre-eminently, and almost to the exclusion of every other thought, the Hebrew prophets were the religious teachers of the nation. And in this office they spoke with authority. As Micah declared of himself, and indeed for all his class, when he denounced certain false prophets who aspired to the position of public instructor without the guarantee of a divine illumination: "But truly I am full of power, by the Spirit of the Lord and of judgment and of might, to declare unto Jacob his transgression and unto Israel his sin." Power, judgment and might by the Spirit, to declare and to rebuke, this was essentially the prophetic gift.

We have no evidence, however, that they ever scattered over the land to proclaim and expound, as do modern Christian pastors. Sometimes singly, sometimes in masses, they spoke, when the Spirit moved, and to such congregations as were at hand and would listen. Though often concerning themselves with personal wrongs or merely local evils, they were wont to appeal in general, not so much to the individual as to the national conscience. Most of the prophecies that have come down to us, bear directly upon the national life. They are applications of the prophetic theology and ethics, uttered with authority, to current political events. Neither prophet, priest nor king were spared. Did David sin, Nathan was ready with his parable of the ewe lamb, and his searching "Thou art the man!" Did Solomon exchange his wisdom for folly, and burden his kingdom with profligacy and extravagance, Abijah clothed himself in a new garment and meeting the ambitious Jeroboam in a field alone, rent his robe into twelve pieces: "Take thee ten pieces, for thus saith the Lord the God of Israel, 'Behold, I will rend the kingdom out of the hand of Solomon and will give ten tribes to thee.'" And Jeroboam, when his day of prosperity came, no sooner reared his golden calf, than lo! there went forth from Judah a prophet to cry against his altar, and to defy him to his face.

That the vast political power involved in such an office was used moderately and wisely, and seldom if ever abused, furnishes extraordinary evidence of the fidelity of these simple and sublime characters to the fundamental idea of prophecy as it has just been defined. The weight of the Seers' influence, whenever the balance in Jewish history trembled, invariably fell upon the scale of sound theology, spiritual worship and pure morality.

The theology of the prophets was very simple. They held to the Unity and Spirituality of God; to His Providence, His Justice and

His Compassion. Surrounded by idolaters among the national enemies, and by perverts to heathenism among the Chosen People, they never failed to discern clearly all that Nature at her best can tell us of Deity; and to this they added a most emphatic and authoritative declaration of the Divine Mercy. Probably no men however gifted, before or since, have had clearer intuition of the moral and religious order of the Universe.

When the truth of their utterances was questioned, or the authoritative tone of its declaration was challenged, they simply appealed to that mysterious something within them which compelled to speech. They were "men of the Spirit," and had no option in the matter. It was Jehovah's breath (*ruah*) in them which uttered the fatal words.

Hence Hebrews never became prophets from mere choice, as youths now enter the ministry. They were called. There was a vision, as of the Throne in the Temple to Isaiah; or a voice, as with the child Samuel; or at least an intense conviction. The call of the Lord now rang in the ear of the designated one, day and night. If with Moses, he said, "O Lord! I am not eloquent, I am slow of speech and of a slow tongue," the Lord seemed to answer, "I will be with thy mouth, and teach thee what thou shalt say." If he moaned with Jeremiah, "O Lord God, behold I can not speak, for I am a child"; the Lord would seem to stretch forth hands to touch his mouth,—" Behold, I have put my words in thy mouth!" And if afterward, amid perils and heartsick, he shrank back, saying with the tearful prophet, "I will not make mention of Him, nor speak any more in His name"; then God's Word was in his heart "as a fire shut up in his bones," and he was "weary with forbearing and could not stay." This intense conviction of a divine call came at times upon men who had not received the slightest education; as in the case of Amos, who was a poor shepherd of Tekoah.

In some cases, the divine afflatus was a constant energy, as with Elijah, Isaiah and Jeremiah; and the prophet was ready to speak the Word of the Lord on all occasions. In other cases it was infrequent, or at least variable in intensity, as when the aged Miriam broke forth into her song of triumph on the shores of the Red Sea, or Deborah rejoiced over the fall of Sisera, or Hannah praised God for a great mercy. Sometimes, even with the greatest Seers, for extraordinary efforts, the Spirit must needs be courted and the divine phrensy aroused by strains of music, as with Elisha at the battle in the desert.

The illumination of the Hebrew prophets was pictorial and ecstatic, and thus in harmony with prevailing habits of thought. At times the Word of the Lord came in a dream, or again it came during trance in a vision. Hence the use of the term Seer. Indeed so wonted was this aspect of their work, that the idea of vision attached itself to the simplest declarative utterances. It is evident that even their general apprehension of religious things was conceived of as a supernatural insight. But even when their words were mere exhortation, their manner of speech was impassioned, and sometimes almost phrensied. This is perhaps hinted at in the term *nabi*, which comes from a root meaning "bubbling" or "boiling." The Spirit of Jehovah so filled the prophet, that in its irrepressible vivacity it effervesced. This effervescence was at times so lively that there resulted only involuntary and unintelligible phrensy.

Yet notwithstanding the overmastering nature of the divine afflation, the individuality of the prophet was never obscured for a moment. No personalities in history are more intense than those of Elijah, Isaiah and Jeremiah. These were men of genius, chosen because they were such. Their characters were stamped upon their words and works. The hopeful and sublime strains of Isaiah are as different from the plaintive notes of Jeremiah, as the stately imagery of "Paradise Lost" from the tearful tenderness of "In Memoriam." The Hebrew prophets were, in general, men of real and often very great ability, swayed by a power from above, of which they were perfectly conscious, but which they neither could long resist nor fully explain.

And no one will deny that such characters as Moses, Samuel, David, Elijah and Isaiah are among the most majestic figures in human history.

Only a small portion of the sayings of these remarkable men has come down to us; but enough survives to awaken the keenest interest in their lives, the gravest patience in listening to their claims and the liveliest admiration for their heroism in deed and eloquence in word. Whatever is rich, tender and grand in our Old Testament has come from them, whether in narrative or appeal. So far as grace and vigor of style are concerned, the most captious criticism of to-day finds little to condemn and much to praise. Bossuet was drawn to the Bible, to religion and to the pulpit by a glance at an' opened chapter of Isaiah: Edmund Burke therein also refreshed his own splendid imagination. In all modern times genius, studying the Hebrew prophets, has found itself face to

face with something nobler even than genius,—
a genius inspired.

And the conclusion is pressing, that either
these men were the victims of a gigantic illusion—an illusion that successive ages only intensified—or that they rightfully spoke with an
authority which no mere genius can claim. The
patient, reverent and spiritual inquirer, however
rationalizing his tendencies may be, will not
long hesitate in decision. If Hebrew prophecy
were an illusion, history surely records no folly
so beneficent, so felicitous, so sublime.

CHAPTER X.

THE UNEXPECTED CHRIST.

' O blessed Well of Love, O Flowre of Grace!
   O glorious Morning Star! O Lampe of Light!
Most lively Image of thy Father's Face!
   Eternal King of Glorie! Lord of Light!
   Meek Lambe of God, before all worlds behight,
How can we thee requite for all this good!
Or what can prize, that thy most precious blood?"
                                 —EDMUND SPENSER.

THE inspired genius of the Hebrew Seers had seemingly exhausted itself, when, after a long silence, there appeared suddenly among the Jewish people a Prophet of superlative illumination.

Many gifted men had gone before Him, in that thorny road of prophetic instruction and heroic devotion; but He was unique, something unpremeditated, a new type of genius, a Master Original. He was a surprise to the world. Even His enemies acknowledged that "never man spake like this man," and it is not to be wondered at, that His disciples, in their annals of His life, picture Him as the Light of the World, the Life of Men and the Word of God.

He has very naturally been compared with Socrates, Confucius, Zoroaster, Gautama and others; but it is interesting to notice that these men of exalted character and wonderful wisdom seem great in proportion as they are like Him. He was peerless, in the judgment of all historians and of all religious critics, the standard of measurement for the prophets of every nation and age.

In dealing with this great historical character, we are approaching a problem of rarest complexity and profundity.

And it seems wise to begin our study by concentrating attention upon the unexpectedness of Christ's career, and the entire originality of His character, words and work. We must forget our familiarity with Christian types of virtue and lines of thought, and put ourselves among the intelligent contemporaries of the Jewish Teacher, so that, if possible, we may receive the striking first impression of Jesus upon His age. So positioned, we shall perceive that He was not a mere outgrowth of His times, but unexpected, alone and, on the groundwork of ordinary conditions, impossible.

We are aware that this assertion is boldly denied by many bright and earnest minds, who, being accustomed to the summary methods of physical science and of historical criticism, think to resolve Jesus of Nazareth, to account for Him and to explain Him into what is deemed His proper place in the story of human progress.

The theories that have been elaborated for the purpose of rationalizing the Prophet of Galilee have been many and contradictory, always changing and very evanescent.

The lasting substance of them may be briefly stated.

In all such attempts, it is in general claimed that the times were such and the circumstances such, that a Jesus Messiah was, in the year of Our Lord one, not only a possibility, but a probability. Jesus, it is said, was a Hebrew prophet, like Elisha or Isaiah, of unequalled power,—but carried away by His own enthusiasm, tyrannized over by His own great thoughts, the victim of ideas the natural product of His times, whose life has suffered gross exaggeration and misconception at the hand of biographers. Such, in brief, is modern Rationalism, as it essays the problem of Christ.

But explanations of this sort ignore a number of facts, to which we address ourselves.

It is not true that Jesus Christ was, in any ordinary sense, an outgrowth of His times. No possible ingenuity can so account for His character and history. Let those portions of the

Gospels which the more earnest of Rationalists have questioned be thrown aside, let Jesus be stripped of all adornment of miraculous power, nay, view Him as one might Socrates, Confucius and Mohammed, and still He can not be explained on the groundwork of those particular and universal influences which ordinarily shape human experience and character.

The more we scrutinize the facts, the more are we impressed with the contrast between the Messiah whom the Jews were expecting and the Christ that came.

The Hebrews, from the beginning, had been a people of ardent religious yearnings. They had ever been wont to expect, with almost boyish enthusiasm, the actual realization in the national life of great popular ideals. Their government was purely theoretic: Jehovah was recognized as King; and the ruler in the palace, to whom pertained the baubles of power, was only His vicegerent. Temporal affairs and spiritual ardors were thus strangely blended in the national history. The people believed that their sins were the only obstacle to a faultless reign and a happy and holy national life. Out of their sense of guilt, out of their broken hopes, out of their intense religious ambition, there arose the idea of a coming Anointed One, who was to realize all temporal and spiritual aspirations and to wield all temporal and spiritual power and authority, not only over Zion, but over all the earth, a Mightiest of prophets, a Priest of priests, a King of kings. These popular aspirations rose and fell, narrowed and widened, became lustrous or dim, according to circumstances and the religious warmth of the times: they formed great tides of spirituality, now filling the popular thought up to highest water-mark of expectancy, and again leaving bare weed-covered shoals and sunken rocks of hopeless unbelief. In certain natures such anticipations had always been pure and elevating; with the masses they were seldom other than dreams of conquest and glory, though even in the latter case the intense religiousness of the Jewish race was always deeply involved. The Messiah expected, and to all appearances needed, was a second David, a man of war, who could both fight and rule,—a priest and holy,—but pre-eminently a magnificent despot, whose kingdom should be visible and terrible, with brave Jews for legionaries and Scribes and Pharisees for councillors.

When Jesus was born at Bethlehem, the tide of Messianic expectation was at its flood. The people were eagerly waiting. It seemed, indeed, "the latter times," a very "Day of Jehovah," "a day of darkness and of gloominess, a day of clouds and of thick darkness." Zion, the beautiful city, lay desolate in the ravishing grasp of Rome; a citadel, occupied by legionaries, overlooked the sacred precincts of the Temple; massacres of Jews by Gentiles were constantly occurring in the towns of Galilee; and all the ills of conquest and misrule vexed the Land. The suffering people argued: that the vials of the wrath of God must have poured forth their utmost contents. A great body of Jewish citizens were calling on God, in agony of spirit, day and night. Surely Zion would soon arise from the dust and put on her beautiful garments and shine! It was a period of illusion. Men deeming themselves watchmen on the walls, now and again fancied that they heard the footfalls upon the mountains of the heralds that were coming with glad tidings to publish peace. In vision they saw Messiah in His glory rise up a power in the land, they beheld the gathering armies, the glorious warfare, the overthrow of Roman legions, the breaking up of Gentile nations, and the supremacy of Jerusalem from the River unto the ends of the earth. In the eagerness of their expectation and the assurance of their hope, they looked upon their oppressors with ravenous, exulting eyes, as though already fallen beneath their heel.

Just then came John the Baptist from the

wilderness, preaching repentance. At once flashed from fervent lips the yearning query: "Who art thou? Art thou the Christ?" And when John declared that he was the Forerunner, and that the "Kingdom" was "at hand," none were surprised. Were they not ready for these things? Had not "the fulness of the times" come?

The Rationalists are thus quite right in claiming that the age demanded a Christ, and that nothing was more natural than that at such a time a Christ should appear. Men attempting to play that *rôle* did come upon the scene. Two such are alluded to in the book of Acts, Theudas and Judas, both of whom seemed to have been ambitious to meet the national desire. Josephus mentioned others. These men were the natural and proper outgrowths of the soil. They tried to deliver Zion by the sword, and so to realize what was universally the orthodox idea of the Messianic glory. Up to the very overthrow of Jerusalem, the land was disturbed by these attempts.

And had Jesus been such a one as Theudas or Judas, the Rationalists would be right, and Christ but the natural fruit of His times.

But undeniably far other was the Son of Man. In every respect He was just what the people did not expect, just what even the scholars and the devout least could understand. Explain them as you will, He possessed the most varied and wonderful powers. Dismissing the question whether He miraculously healed the sick and raised the dead, not even the most skeptical will deny Him the largest mental capacity, insight extraordinary, the most powerful imagination, and a perfect subjection of physical desires to the supremacy of will. His grasp upon other men was so magnetic and irresistible, that at a word they left business and friends and became His disciples, willing to die for love of Him and of His cause. Had He robed Himself in purple at the head of the Messianic party, His would not likely have been the fate of Theudas, who was slain with his four hundred, nor that of Judas of Galilee, who perished with much people; Jesus of Nazareth, if go down He must before the eagles of Rome, would have fallen in the last and best blood of Israel, and His extinction would have been the extinction of the national life. Were the rationalistic hypotheses true, Christ, when He became conscious of His extraordinary powers, would have at least made such an effort. It is recorded, that at this very crisis of self-discovery in His career He was so tempted to do; and at least once the people afforded Him the best of excuses for ambition, by seeking forcibly to crown Him as their king, and to compel Him to take to arms.

Jesus sternly hushed the voice of the Tempter, and persistently evaded and forbade the disloyal adulation of the crowd. Though boldly claiming to be Messiah, He dashed every national hope by declaring that the "Kingdom" foretold for ages was a purely spiritual reign of righteousness. "The Kingdom of God is within you." "My Kingdom is not of this world." One can well imagine the popular disappointment and disgust at such announcements, and well understand the motive of the people in attempting to force the powerful Prophet into some overt act of treason against the Roman Empire that might necessitate a resort to arms and a reversion to the prevalent Messianic ideas of the day. Were all the glowing words of prophecy, and the long and bitter yearning of the past, to come to naught? Were Messiah, then, nothing more than a King of hearts, and His kingdom but repentance, faith and love? Were there to be no overthrow of Romans, no golden sceptre for Jews, no rod of iron for Gentiles? They would not believe it. Surely He was only preparing the way, soon He would throw off this unseemly mask, assume royalty and defy His enemies. But stay! what says He now? "Love your enemies, bless them that curse you, do good to them that hate you, and pray for them which despitefully use you and persecute you!" Love the Romans! bless the Samaritans! Pray for Pilate and his hirelings!

And see how He walks through the cornfields, plucking the ears of grain on the Sabbath day, and how, in the very synagogue, He heals the withered hand. Shades of Moses and of the prophets rise from your graves as He says, "the Son of Man is Lord even of the Sabbath day!"

The righteous stood aghast at what seemed His profanations of holy things. With one wave of the hand He set aside the Rabbinical lore which had clustered around the Jewish Scriptures and now was dear to every class of the people. "Not that which entereth into the mouth defileth a man." "Ye have heard that it hath been said by them of old time—but *I* say unto you." Even the Temple seemed menaced; "but I say unto you, that in this place is one greater than the Temple."

The people believed that a sudden and awful death was a manifest judgment of God upon some peculiar wickedness; but on one occasion, when some were present that told Him of the Galilæans whose blood Pilate had mingled with their sacrifices, Jesus queried, "Suppose ye that these Galilæans were sinners above all the Galilæans because they suffered such things? I tell you nay, but except ye repent, ye shall all likewise perish. Or those eighteen, upon whom the Tower in Siloam fell and slew them, think ye that they were sinners above all men that dwell in Jerusalem? I tell you nay! but except ye repent, ye shall all likewise perish." Thus He attacked their superstitions. Not less mercy did He show the national prejudices. At the very beginning of His ministry He astonished His disciples by preaching a universal religion to some hated and despised Samaritans at the Well of Jacob. Soon after, in His own village of Nazareth, He shocked the self-complacency of the synagogue by declaring " many widows were in Israel in the days of Elias, when the heaven was shut up three years and six months, when great famine was throughout all the land; but unto none of them was Elias sent, save unto Sarepta, a city of Sidon, unto a woman that was a widow. And many lepers were in Israel in the days of Elisha, the prophet; and none of them was cleansed save Naaman the Syrian."

Somewhat later He praised the faith of a Roman Centurion, and turning to His Jewish followers, He added the stinging rebuke: "Verily I say unto you, I have not found so great faith, no, not in Israel"; and then came that grand utterance which no true Jew could seemingly have conceived, much less have uttered: "And I say unto you, that many shall come from the east and the west, and shall sit down with Abraham and Isaac and Jacob in the kingdom of heaven."

Once as they approached a Samaritan village the sectional hostility, which for centuries had built up a wall between Judæa and Samaria, showed itself in a refusal to extend unto Him the rites of hospitality, because forsooth their faces were as though they would go to Jerusalem. James and John, those "Sons of Thunder," full of the ancient prophetic ardor, and swayed by the ancient intolerant spirit, broke forth: "Lord, wilt thou that we command fire to come from heaven and consume them, even as Elias did?" And Jesus showed how little He shared in the feelings of even the purest men of His day by rebuking them: "Ye know not what manner of spirit ye are of! For the Son of Man is not come to destroy men's lives, but to save them."

Once in an assemblage of Jews He wished to inculcate charity and spake a parable to this end. And the hero of the parable was a good *Samaritan!* There were probably not three persons in His audience, outside His own immediate followers, who believed that a Samaritan could be *good* at all. But Jesus saw fit to teach two kinds of charity at once by ascribing benevolence to a heretic. Moreover, in this audacious picture He still farther offended the national self-love by portraying, in contrast, a worthless priest and a worthless Levite.

At a late day, and when His life was in peril, He grieved the patriotic party yet more deeply by boldly advising submission to the powers that were, in His proverb, "Render unto Cæsar the things that are Cæsar's, and unto God the things that are God's."

A striking illustration of the utter difference between the Christ expected and the Christ that came, is to be found in the denunciations of the Pharisees. One is so accustomed to look upon these men as living types of hypocrisy and malice, that it is easily forgotten that they comprised in their ranks the larger part of the devout of their day. Bad as they were, as a class, they represented such religion and such morality as there was in the land. Many of them were earnest, pure-hearted and spotless in life and character. They were pre-eminently the Messianic party, who alone continued to link the Past with the Future. They had been, in days gone by, the Puritans of their times, and their history, in the main, had been interesting and honorable. Formal and heartless as they had become, bad as most of their leaders undoubtedly were, had Jesus been an outgrowth of His day, the Answer to a Need, it is inconceivable that He ever could have been brought to attack them, rather would He have done His utmost to conciliate and win them. He showed that His religious insight was totally different from that of the Rabbis, by hurling at the corrupt ring of Pharisees who controlled things in Jerusalem, a most scathing and terrible indictment.

And at the last, they were priests and scribes who arrested Him, priests and scribes who accused Him before Pilate, priests and scribes who incited the rabble to cry, "Crucify Him!"

But even more significant than this was the awe and perpetual astonishment of those who knew most of His inward life. He was a mystery, and to pure and thoughtful men like Nathaniel and John. He seemed, even to such spiritual natures, high up above them—His thoughts, His purposes and His personality—in the clouds. His own mother, Mary, the most patient, gentle, ardent and spiritual of women, understood Him not, and more than once fell under His rebuke for failing to comprehend. She pondered and waited, and with silent tongue, but wide-open eye and beating heart, followed His sayings and His works to the very hour and place of the Crucifixion. Once her anxiety mastered her reverence, and, with her relatives, at a time when Jesus was followed by great crowds, and at the height of His popularity, she endeavored to reach His person, no doubt to urge Him to rest and to prudence; but Jesus only replied to the summons in His strange, prophetic personality, with the words, "Who is my mother? and who are my brethren?" and He stretched forth His hands toward His disciples, and said: "Behold my mother and my brethren!"

His chosen apostles were in constant perplexity. They enjoyed intimacy with their Lord, but never familiarity. They whispered among themselves about His meanings: they misunderstood, took offence and murmured behind His back. In the storm on the Lake, they scarcely dared awaken Him; and at night, when He met them on the water, they were sore afraid. He led a life by Himself, about which they surmised. Whole nights He spent alone upon mountains, presumably in prayer and meditation. Once He asked them, suddenly, "Whom say men that I, the Son of Man, am?" and the question revealed a great gulf in confidence between Master and disciples. On that last night in which He was betrayed, after a long and tender farewell address, came this tardy acknowledgment: "Lo! now speakest thou plainly and speakest no proverb. Now are we sure that thou knowest all things and needest not that any man should ask thee: by this we believe that thou camest forth from God." And Jesus sadly responded: "Do ye now believe? Behold, the hour cometh, yea, is now come, that ye shall be scattered, every man to his own, and shall leave me alone! And yet I am not alone, because the Father is with me!" These words speak volumes of the loneliness of Christ's inner life all these years. The same appears in the mournful irony of His saying to the drowsy disciples in Gethsemane: "Sleep on now and take your rest! Behold, the hour is at hand, and the Son of Man is betrayed into the hands of sinners."

One memorable night Jesus took His most spiritual apostles with Him up a mountain and gave them a glimpse (in the Transfiguration) of what He was when alone with God; but they could not understand, and were only awestruck and helpless.

It now must be apparent to every candid reader that the rationalistic hypothesis explanatory of Christ is untenable. He was not a product of circumstances. He neither received His call from any recognized existing need nor

His inspiration from popular traditions and hopes. Nay, rather the facts show that Jesus as a character and His life as a mission were alike inconceivable to the human imagination of that day. None but a Christ could have invented a Christ. He was the wonder of His own day. And He has remained the wonder of history. Hundreds of lives of Jesus have been written, viewing Him from many standpoints; but there still remains amazement in every earnest, contemplative mind, and still much to think and to say.

CHAPTER XI.

CHRIST AS AN EPOCH-MAKER.

"Anno Domini!"

NAPOLEON BONAPARTE once said, "Great men are like meteors: they glitter, and are consumed, to enlighten the world." And often is it true that genius is a mere flash in the dark—dazzling, blinding, and soon out. Napoleon himself was a case in point. There is, however, a creative genius that shines like the sun forever, and by its beams illumines, vitalizes, gladdens and beautifies. Such a Light was, and still is, Jesus Christ. His genius, like sunshine, was creative and perpetual. He died to rise again and live forevermore. His brief life turned the world upside down. He established a new Kingdom, He promulgated a new Law, and He introduced a new Civilization. But not as Lycurgus nor as Solon. His Kingdom was simply Righteousness; His Law, the Golden Rule; His Civilization, Justice for all and the Welfare of the greatest number. He treated men as though they were dead and demanded such a moral reform that it should seem like a coming anew to life, a resurrection or a new birth. Himself spotless, He set the standard of human character higher than any moralist ever before had ever conceived of demanding. Pythagoras, Socrates, Gautama, Confucius, and others had forbidden enmity and evil-doing: Christ demanded that one should love his neighbor as himself. He denounced the world for its shams, its follies, its vices and its crimes, and yet showed Himself possessed of the largest faith in the possibilities of human reformation and attainment. Bad as man was, there was nothing he might not become. Though one were a very child of the Devil, he might become the Son of God, the Temple of the Holy Ghost and the Heir of Glory. His humble, ignorant and often dull peasant disciples were princes; and any poor drudge, labor as he must, be weary as he might and afflicted beyond measure, in Him found rest. For with God there was no respect of persons.

Seemingly all this concerned only the religious growth of men; but really it involved thorough revolution in human thinking and action, political, social and moral. It involved revolution, not at once precipitated, but in time inevitable. Indeed, it supplied the germs of all beneficent change.

Glance for a moment at this undermining and creative work of Christ's personality and teachings, in subsequent history.

Christianity struck at the accursed evil of *caste;* which was recognized in the corrupt Judaism of the day. To be sure, nothing was said about slavery or classes in society; but the system provided for their ultimate abolishment in its Golden Rule of Justice and Charity. Before God, the slave was as good as the Emperor, the layman as the priest; and in another world Dives might be in torment and Lazarus in Abraham's bosom.

Christ said nothing against *Tyranny,* yet His Coming was the only terrible and lasting blow that ever has been struck at despotism, and His Sermon on the Mount is to-day the only unanswerable argument for self-government. Seeming to consent to political evils which He could not at once abolish by mere denunciation, Jesus founded a purely democratic Church, a Republic within the Empire, and the very babes were to be considered as in the Covenant—that is, in league with God. The principle of such an organization, open to all and inviting all to membership (or citizenship), was absolutely hostile to every kind of oppression, and was sure, in time,—as it came to be understood and realized,—to work free institutions. Our modern Republics and constitutional governments are founded, not on ancient Greek democracy nor on Roman so-called republicanism, but upon the Church of Christ, with its unrestricted membership and its Golden Rule.

A significant document from the secret archives of the famous "Third Section" of the Russian Despotism has come to light in a German work recently published ("Von Nicolaus I. to Alexander III."), in which Prince Galitzin, Minister of Education, is accused of having introduced the "damnable practice of reading the Bible, which, as is well known, was the origin of the terrible reign of the Jacobins in France. Our servants are already beginning to imagine that they are the equals of their masters"!!

Moreover, Christianity furnished new underlying principles for common and statute *law*, germs to expand and grow and replace, until such time as human jurisprudence should become a very Sermon on the Mount. It provided new sanctions for moral conduct in its Heaven and Hell,—vividly pictured for the rude culture of the age,—and thus gave, not only to the preacher of righteousness, but as well to the magistrate, a new guarantee for good behavior.

Jewish custom licensed *slaughter* of prisoners and *imprecation* upon enemies. Christ not only enjoined mercy and forgiveness; He urged principles that have rendered less frequent, and must in time wholly prevent, wars. Carried out in letter and in spirit, the Faith will break down national barriers, give resistless power to international law and introduce the peaceful reign of universal justice.

Already, through the spread of Christian sentiment, wars between civilized nations are become unprofitable. The conqueror is forbidden now, thanks to Christ, to enslave, rob or maltreat the conquered. If he do so, the whole world cries out shame upon him. Hence wars are nearly as crushing a disaster for the one party as for the other; and the mighty force of self-interest is arrayed to show their folly, and by every device of diplomacy to prevent them.

Jewish custom allowed *polygamy;* and under all existing systems *divorce* was a mere formality. Jesus emphasized the sacredness of the marriage relation, He declared frivolous divorce a crime against God; and He hallowed the home as the very nursery of both piety and morals.

But more radical and more important even than this general revolution, was that wrought on each individual believer who sought and found Christ. Views of life were expanded, the conscience quickened and the whole nature animated with earnestness. The Jews had looked upon life as all, or at least as the most, of existence; the future to them, when not quite a blank, had been very dim and dreary. And Greeks and Romans had dreaded death, as, even in Elysian fields, less to be desired than life. But Jesus declared an Immortality of light, life and bliss. He said that He had come that men might have life and that they might have it more abundantly. This earthly existence was but a preparation, a sojourn in a desert: Heaven was Paradise and Home. Life was a Race: Heaven gave the Crown. Life was a prophecy, a study in faith, a school of discipline for virtue: Heaven was fulfilment, knowledge, perfection.

Christ brought to bear upon the believer a powerful commingling of motives, inclining him not merely to accept His teachings, but, much more, to practice them. Fear, ambition, conscience and aspiration were all appealed to. The head was convinced and the heart touched. And there was offered, of pure grace, blessed influences of the Divine Spirit, to strengthen the feeble will, steady the wavering purpose, convert the depraved heart, and to give assurance of adoption into sonship and guarantee of the glorious liberty of the children of God. Christ's own personality became and has continued a mighty power for good in the believer. History shows nothing else like it. Even to-day there are many millions to declare that it is Christ for them to live and that He is in them the hope of glory.

This present, persistent, all-compelling personality of Jesus appears in our standards of right and wrong and in all our judgments. The very brain-structure of men in general has undergone Christian modification; and we now literally inherit something of Christ as an instinct. Christ is unconsciously become the ideal of character and the teacher of the heart and the standard of criticism for all the civilized world. Even unbelievers in His claims endorse His personality, by constantly quoting Him against what they conceive to be unjust or untrue in particular statements of Christian faith. And when they find, here and there, in this and in that heathen sage, morsels of truth or sentiment of a Christian flavor, they send up a shout of triumph; which is a rare tribute to Jesus.

It has perhaps already occurred to the reader that to Christ has been ascribed what Christianity has done only in the course of ages. But beyond question the glory is Christ's. At first the light shone in darkness, and it is true the darkness comprehended it not; He came unto His own, and His own received Him not.

Something similar has happened to all great illuminations of God-given genius. They have anticipated the final acceptance. The Copernican theory at first was pronounced false, and persecuted by not only the Church, but as well by the Universities. It was true and hence has triumphed, but long after its great discoverer died. Calculus is true, and long has been a useful method of mathematical research; yet how many even of the educated could, off-hand, give any lucid account of it?—the time, however, may come when it will be taught, like Algebra, in the high-schools. Mozart was none the less a musical genius because so few, even of musicians, can appreciate his "Requiem." Cathedrals and paintings, inventions and discoveries are for the few, until they have, by and by, worked into the very brain structure and become part of the mental and emotional machinery of the many. The few hurry on, the many lag after. The truth may at first be obscured: in the end it will prevail and become commonplace.

Christianity illumined the Johns and Stephens and Pauls; but from the beginning the multitude of the disciples lagged far behind the opportunities and privileges of the new faith. Indeed the visible triumph of Christianity was not its real success; and Christendom has never been quite equivalent to the power of Christ in history. Ecclesiastical history is the story of the conflict of the Christian principle with three Titanic foes, Judaism, Imperialism and Barbarism.

Scarcely were the Churches founded ere they were filled with Judaizing believers, and the faith threatened to prove but a petty reform of the ancient Hebrew system of belief and manner of life.

This danger escaped, there came speedily universal triumph and political power. Christianity became the religion of an Empire, and a department of State. A Hierarchy, pervaded by the imperialism of the times, sprang up, and the gentle appeals of Jesus to the spiritual nature became the authoritative thunderings of councils, and His simple methods a gorgeous pageantry.

The Churches, thus corrupted, were put to even severer test in the irruption upon the Roman Empire of barbarians.

In the middle of the third century the Goths had invaded Greece, had sacked Athens and had burned the Temple of Diana at Ephesus.

In the year 410 Alaric, King of the Visigoths, captured and sacked Rome. In 640 the Arabs, under the banner of Mohammed, took possession of Alexandria, and burned the great library of the Ptolemies. So the deluge of barbarism rolled over the ancient seats of learning and culture, till all the world lay a waste of heaving ignorance and cruelty. Learning retreated to monasteries and desert caves. Civilization went into total eclipse. Art and polite literature ceased to be even a possibility. Physical Science, which under the Ptolemies and previously had begun to make encouraging progress, ceased its discoveries. Until the fourteenth century scarcely a work of art was executed in the whole of Europe worthy of preservation; scarce a book was written worthy of perusal; and, except the mariner's compass, not an invention was made worthy of note at the present time. Everything beautiful, elegant or thoughtful in human intelligence long since had been suffocated to death by the black fumes of stupid barbarism. Everything except Christianity. Christ had not ceased to be a vital power in the world. Piety everywhere, in a humble way, flourished. Christianity, essentially missionary, was silently busy all those hard, dark and cruel ages, assimilating the enormous mass of political corruption and barbarism which had been thus rudely thrust into her all-devouring ecclesiastical system. Without doubt Christian institutions failed to bear the strain and became themselves barbarous, and the hierarchy of the Dark Ages undeniably went with civilization into eclipse. But genuine religion survived, and with intense energy strove to leaven the whole crude lump. The force of Christianity for seven centuries was expended in the purely missionary effort to humanize the so-called Christian world.

The Reformation was the first sign given by the Church of the Middle Ages of its assimilation of ancient heathenism and of its latent vitality. And even the Reformation, though an earnest effort to return unto the simplicity of the Master, lacked much of appreciating His wisdom, His charity and the scope of His mission. Indeed we can assert with truthfulness, not that during these eighteen centuries the Church has been Christianizing the world, so much as that Christ has been Christianizing the Church.

And if Inquisitions and Dragoonades and pompous idolatries in ecclesiastical history be referred to, the reply is at hand. The fountain of a river is not responsible for the filth of its tributaries. The Mississippi at St. Louis is laden with mud, but it would be fallacious to argue that therefore the upper waters were foul. The mud comes in on the Missouri. Have patience and those turbid waters will in time drop their sediment, and at last will issue forth pure upon the Gulf of Mexico. Christianity has been fouled by its tributaries, but it will in time issue pure as its original fountain.

CHAPTER XII.

THE TRUTH IN PARABLE.

" The Christian Gospel is pictorial. Its every line or lineament is traced in some image or metaphor. All God's revelation is made to the imagination. And all the rites and services and ceremonies of the ancient time were only a preparation of draperies and figures for what was to come—the basis of words sometime to be used as metaphors of the Christian grace. Christ is God's last metaphor."—HORACE BUSHNELL.

GREAT teachers, who would instruct their kind in new truth, encounter two serious difficulties as to method.

First, there are no words fitted to convey their novelties of thought. The vocabulary of any language represents only what has been conceived and what is still current in the minds of men. Speech comes into being and grows to utter daily needs and to describe customary usages. A man of genius, then, who sees what none but he has yet discovered, and who would tell the world, must coin new words, or else use old ones with a new meaning. In either case, he will seem to say one thing and mean another. Perforce he must use language suggestively, he must talk in parables. The growth of words, in number and in meanings, gives us the entire history of human progress. The loftiest terms were once commonplace. "Tragedy" of old was but a goat song, "comedy" but a village ditty. The word "book" originally designated the bark of the beech-tree, on which our barbarous ancestors scribbled their thoughts. "Scribe" and "scrub" are cousins. "Spirit" once meant simply breath, and "lord" is the Saxon "hlaford"—loaf-giver.

A teacher in new things can only avail himself of this expansiveness in language; and, taking such words as best suit his purpose, he must breathe into them his own inspiration. But this necessity increases greatly the difficulty of making himself understood. In moulding a language he is educating a whole people and providing instinctive knowledge for future generations; and the inertia to be overcome is enormous.

This inertness is increased by a second difficulty, the general inability of men to understand novelties. Using language suggestively, the teacher appeals to the intelligence of his audience; and too often it fails him. The most lucid expositions of unwonted truths and facts fall in general upon dull ears. Francis Galton, the author of a recent but already famous work on hereditary genius, declares of the most cultivated popular audiences that can be assembled in England, that "It often occurs to persons familiar with some scientific subject to hear men and women of mediocre gifts relate to one another what they have picked up about it from some lecture,—say at the Royal Institution,—where they have sat for an hour listening with delighted attention to an admirably lucid account, illustrated by experiments of the most perfect and beautiful character, in all of which they expressed themselves intensely gratified and highly instructed. It is positively painful to hear what they say. Their recollections seem to be a mere chaos of mist and misapprehension, to which some sort of shape and organization has been given by the action of their own pure fancy, although alien to what the lecturer intended to convey." This does not prove that men are in general stupid, but simply that original thinkers are ahead of their times, in both words and meanings, and that they put a severe and unwonted strain upon the average intelligence. The popular understanding as well as the popular intelligence must be educated up to the teacher's level. But this involves difficulty and danger. Says the French writer, Fanin: "Fear of hypocrites and of fools is the great plague of thinking and writing."

Prophets must be content to be misunderstood and misinterpreted, until the growing capacities of mankind take in their revelations; and lucky for them if, ere that hour come, they fall not victims, like Socrates, like Cecco d'Ascoli, like Giordano Bruno, like a thousand others,—to the crudeness of their times.

Is there not something impressive about this hurrying of language after swift thought?— about this eager reaching up of the average intelligence to comprehend the sublimities discovered by genius? Dangerous to the teacher, fraught with difficulties of method for him and yet of such incomparable importance to the world.

And those original men stand highest, who not only think the great thoughts of progress, but who as well stimulate the average mind to take them in. He who knows how to quicken the simplest language, so as through ordinary words to arouse extraordinary thoughts in the multitude, and who braves their prejudice, their ignorance and their passion, that one is to his inmost soul a prophet of the Most High.

But if all this be so of popular instruction in difficult matters, generally considered, how doubly descriptive of the revelation of religious truth. Here, fanatical prejudice is to be overcome, and the language to be moulded anew is already crystallized into hard, exact meanings, sacred to foreordained uses.

Moreover, here, a third difficulty appears. The matters to be treated of lie, in part at least, beyond the possibilities of any language however elaborated, and beyond the full comprehension of any mind however educated. Religious truths are colossal, shadowy, appealing to Faith rather than to Reason, based on Intuition rather than on Logic and incapable of scientific demonstration. They challenge spirituality. When Deity, Providence, Salvation and Immortality are the themes, words reel under their crushing load. It is simply impossible to compress the infinities of the supernatural world into definitions and formulas. Exact statements exclude the larger part. It is as though a man should attempt to frame in all space or to perfect chronology for all time. The poetic, mystical utterance of the prophet, faulty as it ever must be, is far better than the prosaic theorems of the philosopher and theologian. The attitude of mind in which religious truth is contemplated is not analytic, but intuitive. And the faculty ultimately appealed to is that faith which underlies reason.

Hence all religious teachers have been men of wit and imagination, who spoke not in definitions, but in parables; who, in their vain struggle to find expression through their own words and understanding in their listeners, ever have meant far more and other than they literally said.

Take Plato's description of God: "Truth is His body and light His shadow!" It would be a curious intelligence that could pronounce this gem of thought literally exact; yet in its poetic suggestiveness it bears an infinitude of sublime reflection. An archangel might have said it, and still have had occasion to ponder.

Much of former belief has come down to us in dark hints, mystic sayings and curious symbols. Indeed, it is hard to decide as to the highest attainments of the ancients; for the very reason that their beliefs were only for the initiated and uttered in imagery of word and act.

Of all religious teachers, Jesus Christ, from the nature of the case, encountered the accumulated difficulties of divine instruction in largest measure. His ideas were not only new, but of infinite vastness of being and range, reaching not only beyond the conveniences of the languages of His day, but beyond the very possibilities of any language, and not only hard to conceive of, but forever destined to involve perilous sublimities of thought. Both the popular speech and the popular understanding failed Him; and it directly appeared that, in part, speech and understanding must ever prove insufficient.

There was but the one method available. He could only speak suggestively, using low words with high meanings and pictures instead of essays, forever throwing Himself upon the intelligent spirituality of the devout. This He did: daring ignorance and prejudice, He appealed to spirituality. Casting off the old scholastic terms or using them in an astonishingly new way, He spoke in "parables"—for the Greek term parable means any kind of pictorial indirection; and we are told, "Without a parable spake He not unto them."

Thus He dealt largely in metaphors. He was the Vine, Bread from Heaven and Fountain of Life, Shepherd and Master. To become His disciple was Creation and Newbirth. Holiness was Life Eternal. His Gospel taught the Way.

He frequently used comparisons. The Kingdom of Heaven was like a Net, like Sowing, like seeking a lost coin or purchasing a goodly pearl.

Sometimes His analogies of thought were expressed by the same words for either term, but in different meanings, and there resulted all the freshness, though none of the vulgarity, of a pun; as in His description of the mystery of conversion: "The wind (pneuma) bloweth where it listeth, and thou hearest the sound thereof and canst not tell whence it cometh and whither it goeth. So is every one that is born of the Spirit (Pneuma)," where the same term (whether spoken in Greek or Aramaic—pneuma or ruah) is used in a lower and a higher significance, with the effect of rendering vivid the comparison. This solemn playing upon words was quite a favorite figure of speech with the ancient Hebrew prophets.

Jesus delighted in contrasts. On one occasion He said: "Think not that I am come to destroy the Law!" and He emphasized His declaration intensely. But at once He added of that class who most rigidly kept the Law: "Except your righteousness shall exceed the righteousness of the scribes and Pharisees, ye shall in no case enter into the Kingdom of Heaven." He vividly portrayed God's love, not by comparing it with a parent's fondness, but by a contrast: "If ye then being evil, know how to give good gifts unto your children, how much more will your Father, which is in Heaven, give good things to them that ask Him!" The parable of the Unjust Judge is an intense contrast, its power lying in the utter unlikeness of the two terms, the thought being: "If an unjust judge, for the mere importunity of an insignificant suppliant teasing him with a bad, or at least commonplace, motive, should be brought to do his official duty, how much more a thousandfold will the just God listen to the reasonable cry of His dear children?"

Jesus did not despise hyperbole. "It is easier for a camel to go through the eye of a needle than for a rich man to enter into the Kingdom of God."

Mark His effectiveness in irony. He would turn from the Pharisees with some such pungent remark as: "They that be whole need not a physician, but they that are sick. . . . . I came not to call the righteous, but sinners to repentance." "I say unto you, that likewise joy shall be in Heaven over one sinner that repenteth more than over ninety and nine just persons that need no repentance." It was irony when He said, in gentle rebuke to His drowsy disciples, on that last night in Gethsemane: "Sleep on now and take your rest: behold the Hour is at hand and the Son of Man is betrayed into the hand of sinners." There was an ironical lesson to His narrow-minded followers in His seemingly cruel remarks to the Syrophenician woman who followed Him and besought Him to heal her daughter. The Master was at once testing her faith and uttering their bigotry in the words: "I am not sent but unto the lost sheep of the House of Israel!" "It is not meet to take the children's bread and cast it to dogs!" And what else but saddest irony, borrowed from Isaiah, was that mournful utterance: "By hearing ye shall hear and shall not understand; and seeing, ye shall see and shall not perceive. For this people's heart is waxed gross and their ears are dull of hearing and their eyes they have closed, lest at any time they should see with their eyes and hear with their ears and should understand with their heart and should be converted and I should heal them!"

Still more noteworthy were His parables proper—as of the Prodigal Son, of the Pharisee and the Publican, or of the Rich Man and Lazarus.

And not only in set speech did He teach by images and pictures, His most ordinary conversation was in riddles. Did an over-zealous, light-hearted and empty-headed fellow come running to Him with a breathless and thoughtless "I will follow Thee whithersoever Thou goest!" he was calmed down to ponder over these words: "Foxes have holes and birds of the air have nests, but the Son of Man hath not where to lay His head!" Did a really earnest man make excuses when commanded to follow Him, "Lord, suffer me first to go and bury my father!" he was curtly bidden, "Let the dead bury their dead; but go thou and preach the Kingdom of God."

Nor was Jesus content with indirection of speech, public and private. He taught also in vivid pantomime. He acted parables, as in breaking bread and feeding the five thousand, as in washing His disciples' feet and in driving the traders from the Temple. Indeed, His every miracle was a pictorial sermon on faith, an object-lesson in righteousness. How vividly true was this of His miraculous healings. Every reader of the Word must have noticed that in general, if not always, He insisted upon "faith" as a condition to the exercise of His beneficent power. This He did, not that He could not work the deed of mercy without some particular subjective state of mind in the patient, but seemingly because His ministry as a physician was purposely subordinated to the great end of Salvation. Every miraculous healing kept before the people in connection three things: the Disease, the Physician and Saving Faith. The disease was not sin, the physician not necessarily a savior of souls, and the faith demanded was not what the Christian religion afterward required; but the former typified the latter. In this way Jesus familiarized the people with the idea of salvation by faith, and prepared the way for the great dogma of Justification. His very life accommodated itself to the urgent necessities of the situation. The Temptation, the Transfiguration, the Crucifixion, the Resurrection and the Ascension, were all, apart from this historical or doctrinal meaning, vastly effective as divine parables for the instruction of the world, and so used by His apostles, notably by Paul.

The *dogmas* of Christianity were all pictorial, and never, at least by Jesus, scientifically expressed. To become a Christian was—viewed on the human side—to " change purpose," to become " as a little child," to " writhe ($αγωνιζομαι$) into the strait gate"; while from the divine side it was to be " born again of water and of the Spirit," to be " new created in Christ Jesus." Virtue was described as Love. Heaven was Abraham's Bosom, or Paradise, or My Father's House; and Hell was Gehenna—the moral refuse heap of the world. The relation of Jesus to the Father was Sonship, and His pre-existence was asserted in the enigmatic phrase, " Before Abraham was, I am." Atonement was simply described as somehow vicarious. Jesus was the Shepherd, who gave His life for the sheep.

His blood was shed for the remission of sins. Like the brazen serpent in the Wilderness He must be lifted up on the Cross—though no real serpent—for the healing of those who were bitten of the serpent of sin. He was Saviour of the World; and whosoever believed in Him should not perish, but have everlasting life.

In short, the great dogmas were from Beyond, and though revealed were still on the Outermost Rim of human thought.

Doubtless by thus speaking in parables Christ subserved some of the ordinary ends of pictorial discourse.

He winnowed thereby His audience. The difficulty in understanding drove away the gaping senseless crowd, who ever were ready to go out after a new Messiah, who shouting one day "Hosanna!" were ready on the morrow to join in the cry of "Crucify him!" To such His veiled Spirituality was displeasing. What these wanted were loaves and fishes, miracles, battles and spoils. Jesus, through His parables, was soon rid of them. A marked instance of this occurred after His discourse at Capernaum, where He told them that they must eat His flesh and drink His blood, to their very great disgust. Only the thoughtful could have patience to follow His subtle meanings with docility and spiritual insight.

Moreover, for such as would listen, what He said and did was more easily and correctly *remembered* for being pictorial. His words were darts, with point of steel and tipped with feathers of blue and gold. At what they were aimed, there they struck; and where they struck they pierced, and where they pierced they stayed. They had what Howells declares the essential properties of a good proverb, "Sense, shortness and salt." Or, to borrow a still more apt illustration from an old Latin description of a good epigram, they were like bees, small and sweet, but with a sting in the tail. This was of utmost importance, as there was no one present with pencil and note-book to jot down directly His sayings and doings, and no printing-presses to secure an exact preservation of what memoirs were ultimately written. His pithy sayings once heard, even though misunderstood at the time, were easily remembered; while His vivid parabolic pictures and attitudes were never to be forgotten. In every word and action there lived the very soul of wit, and wit is immortal. Hence even we of to-day know to a certainty that He uttered these things, without any learned work on Evidences; for none other could have invented them.

But granting these subordinate ends, we are

only on the surface of the matter. Christ, besides these considerations of utility, was acting under that higher necessity of which we have spoken. Imagery, and because suggestive rather than descriptive, formed the proper language of His thought.

Once His disciples asked Him: "Why speakest Thou unto them in parables?" And He replied to themselves in riddles: "Because it is given unto you to know the mysteries of the Kingdom, but to them it is not given. For whosoever hath, to him shall be given, and he shall have more abundance; but whosoever hath not, from him shall be taken away even that he hath. Therefore speak I to them in parables; because they seeing see not, and hearing they hear not, neither do they understand." It will be noticed that this very compliment to their superior capacity to understand direct teaching of profound things is couched in highly indirect and almost mystical language. It certainly did not ascribe to the disciples any insight which lifted them above the necessity upon which we are dwelling. It simply meant that they needed less stimulation than the multitude, with whom anything like categorical statements of the "mysteries of the Kingdom" was entirely out of the question. Men could be shown divine things only according as they already had spirituality of discernment and understanding; just as, in business, men made money who had capital to trade upon.

Indeed, it is very significant of the peculiar difficulties and perils which beset Christ as a religious teacher, that the very Apostles, selected doubtless for their peculiar docility and spirituality, were constantly failing in comprehension, murmuring aside, whispering in a corner, and doubting, even up to the day of Pentecost.

In this very suggestiveness lay the superlative value of all Christ's teachings. The most spiritual men never have been able nor are now able to exhaust His meanings. Take His simple and sublime "God is a Spirit, and they that worship Him must worship Him in spirit and in truth." That will be a theme for loftiest genius to muse upon ten thousand years hence. Or the dogma, "God is love." The word love here is crushed under its burden, and must grow large and strong with the ages in order to bear up. Jesus bade us pray, "Our Father." This was a parable. It could not have been technical description, for God is not our father literally. It could not have been figuratively exact, for we have learned that to Christ parental love was but a poor contrast to the infinite Mercy. There is a limit to even a father's solicitude, and many parents are unjust and cruel. The phrase, however, admirably served the purposes of suggestion. It set men thinking. The analogy was only a crutch, which, as the limb strengthened, might be thrown away. So of all the picture-lessons, proverbs, sarcasms, riddles and dogmas uttered by Jesus. They were hints, symbols, aids to religious reflection, appeals to spirituality.

The Kingdom of Heaven was, indeed, like a sower going forth to sow, and planting seed and leaving it to the sunshine and the rain, well knowing that only in good soil would it bring forth abundantly.

Hence the frequent warnings uttered by the Master, calling His listeners to heedful attention. As the oft-repeated, "He that hath ears to hear, let him hear!" Once He said to His disciples in encouragement, "Blessed are your eyes, for they see: and your ears, for they hear." On one occasion a certain woman loudly declared, happy the mother who had borne such a Son: Jesus replied, pointedly, "Yea, rather blessed are they that hear the Word and keep it." Such declarations as these were frequent on the lips of Jesus: "Ye shall know the truth, and the truth shall make you free." "The words that I speak unto you, they are spirit and they are life."

We are thus called to contemplate a fact of utmost importance, not only as regards all religious truth, but especially as concerns the teachings of Jesus and the dogmas of Christianity. And the reader will not unreasonably demand to know its bearing.

Some would have it that our Bible becomes a sort of Chinese puzzle for ingenuity to pick out, a magic mirror or a crystal globe in which conjurors can discern the signs of the times and predict the future Millennium and the Second Advent—a land of dreams in which the imagination may run riot at will.

Nothing, however, could be further from the truth. Jesus was intensely, and even unto death, in earnest. It would be quite impossible to show that He ever uttered one syllable for mere curiosity to puzzle over, or pictured one symbol for mere ingenuity to decipher. The parables of righteousness lend themselves to no purpose of divination, and appeal only to spirituality.

It certainly does result from this great fact upon which attention has been fixed: that creeds, however well they may temporarily serve certain purposes, must be ever very imperfect either for profound or for lasting expression of dogmatic truth.

Moreover, this great fact that Jesus spoke in

parables forever deprives dogmatism of logical standing-room. Dogmatism and persecution thrive only on such hard and fast and narrow statements as can be used for standards of judgment and condemnation. A truth which needs spirituality to discern its meaning can never become a reasonable ground for anathemas, thumb-screws and the stake.

But pre-eminently the lesson of the great fact is the thesis of this entire treatise. Divine things, though clearly revealed, need patience, reverence and spirituality.

CHAPTER XIII.

THE AUTHORITY OF CHRIST.

" Jesus Christ is not only, as many at the present day would have it, a great question: He is far rather the divine Answer to all human questions and complaints. If we look at Him merely as a question, He becomes more and more unintelligible."—CHRISTLIEB.

IF, in this chapter, we question the authority of Jesus as Teacher and Saviour of Men, it will be only that He Himself may answer.

Christ declared His inspiration prophetic and His authority absolute as the truth itself.

"I came forth from the Father." "Whom He hath sent, Him ye believe not." "My doctrine is not mine, but His that sent me." "As my Father hath taught me I speak these things." "I have not spoken of myself, but the Father which sent me, He gave me a commandment, what I should say and what I should speak. . . . . Whatsoever I speak, therefore, even as the Father said unto me, so I speak." "The Word which ye hear is not mine, but the Father's which sent me." Like the Hebrew prophets of old, He was a Mouthpiece of Jehovah, a "Man of the Spirit."

It is customary in Apologetic Theology to base the argument for the validity of Christian revelation upon Christ's miracles. Doubtless these served as divine vouchers during His lifetime and did much to give to the new religion a vigorous start. It may be fairly questioned, however, whether the old method is equally available with the skeptics of to-day. The difficulty of proving that the miracles actually occurred in the face of modern Biblical criticism and of the hostile attitude of science has become very great. Nay, rather a strange reversion of method is impending, and the miracles instead of guaranteeing Christ are likely to be themselves accepted only on the authority of Christ.

This is not to be regretted. It brings us to the heart of the matter. Jesus of Nazareth, as a Divine Teacher and Saviour, must, in the last analysis, appeal to the minds and hearts of men on the strength of Himself. What He said and was for all mankind must form the challenge to spirituality. His Revelation, His Mission, Himself, all taken in their unity and simplicity as one Religious Phenomenon, must be accepted or rejected on inherent merit.

Jesus laid great stress upon the mind-quickening and soul-convicting power of what He in various ways revealed. The Truth carried its own conclusiveness.

"The words that I speak unto you, they are spirit and they are life." He considered His system of truth so persuasive and irresistible, that men who rejected it thereby condemned themselves. "If any man hear and believe not, I judge him not, for I came not to judge the world, but to save the world. He that rejecteth me and receiveth not my words hath one that judgeth him: the Word that I have spoken, the same shall judge him in the last day. For I have not spoken of myself." Jesus herein, as elsewhere, appealed to His teachings as being not the speculations of a philosopher, but self-evidently the eternal truth. He spake from God to the religious nature. Hence there can be no authoritative go-between, no final pope, council nor creed. The inmost soul must decide upon His claims.

This showed a truly marvellous faith in the capacity of the human soul to appreciate vital truth; and yet did not go beyond the provable facts of the case.

There is, surely, within us a trustworthy response to religious truth. Joubert has said: "When a nation gives birth to a man who is able to produce a great thought, another is born who is able to understand and admire it." We might enlarge upon this to declare that when God raises up a prophet to utter things from Beyond, there are some ears that will hear and some hearts that will thrill.

Somewhat of an analogy exists between this response of spirituality and æsthetic taste. As there is in every one a certain taste to detect the beautiful and more or less latent; so is there in all an instinctive feeling for the higher kinds of truth, more or less uncultivated. The reason that all men do not feel the entire force of a great dogma of righteousness, on first presentation, is that the inner sense referred to, like æsthetic taste, is in general rude and untrained.

The tenderness and exalted sentiment of a great poem are not apparent to a child's mind, nor to any but those who have refined their natures into sympathy with the poet's enthusiasm; and the more one studies a masterpiece of poetic art, the more of touching and original thought is discovered. The study of art expands the inner response to the beautiful.

Go for the first time into a gallery of ancient paintings. You pass rapidly along, your eye glancing over the dingy surfaces of great squares of canvas. A comical beggar-boy by Murillo, a Flora by Titian or a group of Nymphs by Giordano arrests attention. The grosser beauties of art are perceived at once, but the great themes are passed by unnoticed. You look into your guide-book for the more famous pieces, and lo, a double-starred Raphael! Strange you had passed it by! How old it is! how faded! how homely! Only a St. Cæcilia, in peasant garb and with uplifted seraphic face, and earnest men to right and left. Few lines, few colors and no slightest trace of either manly or womanly charm of sense! Yet somehow you like the picture, the face of the maid is so pure, sweet and spiritual, and her devotion so genuine; and on the scarred and wrinkled visages of the men there appears a manhood so Christly. You sit down to study this work. It grows upon you. You go away and come again. You gaze and ponder and by and by you wonder. The picture begins to fascinate you. You find yourself worshipping with St. Cæcilia; you feel the thrill of her rapture; you resent the careless tread of tourists passing by; you scarce dare breathe, lest her adoration be marred. Great thoughts now come into the mind, new feelings stir in the heart. You have communed with Raphael, you have begun to do homage to the true greatness of art. And at last you reluctantly bid farewell to the gallery, wondering that you could ever have preferred Floras and Nymphs and have passed by undetected so superb a creation of genius. Henceforth you will study paintings with a new sense.

Now something like this occurs in listening to the revelations of prophetic natures. If we will ponder we may understand. The sense grows with use.

Doubtless this sense has its limits. Many spiritual truths from Beyond might be revealed, which it could not test. It is adapted to apprehend and feel only such dogmas as have been or are likely to be revealed to mankind.

And these not intricately. It is never absolutely unerring, and hence can have no excuse for being dogmatic. It is a general recognition and not a scientific analysis. Across the ages it detects in Christ the Divine: it hears, hearkens, bends the knee, bows the head, believes, adores and obeys.

Probably every earnest disciple of Jesus has been conscious of a growth like this, in years of study on the Bible and of reflection on Christian doctrine. No one can listen to Christ's words, in a teachable spirit, without being deeply moved and irresistibly urged on toward conviction. Probably no one has ever gone to Our Saviour, with the honest intention of giving Him a fair hearing, who has not been carried on from point to point, until the grandest stretches of divine thought have opened before him. It is not strange that Jesus was so bold in His famous assertion: "If any man will do His will he shall know of the doctrine, whether it be of God or whether I speak of myself!"

This is the formidable argument in favor of Christianity. The words of Christ, with His character as illustration, guarantee His authority. His fulfilment of prediction is of intense interest, and His miraculous deeds of mercy very significant; but the beauty, fitness, goodness and inner conclusiveness of the truth uttered and lived mainly carry conviction.

On that last night, in which He was betrayed, He said to His disciples: "These things I have spoken unto you in proverbs; but the time cometh when I shall no more speak to you in proverbs, but I shall show you plainly of the Father." He could only have meant to promise the coming of the Spirit of Truth to quicken spirituality and to work discernment.

And he to-day who would "know of the doctrine" has no authoritative Church to interpret for him, and no sufficient creed to define, but only the great sayings themselves, a docile heart and the Spirit of Truth.

CHAPTER XIV.

THE MYSTERIES OF CHRIST.

"*For now we see through a mirror, darkly.*"—PAUL.

THE mysterious in Christian doctrine was recognized by Jesus, not only in His method of instruction through parables, as fully set forth in a preceding chapter, but by direct allusion. On one occasion He said to His disciples: "To you it is given to know *the mysteries* of the Kingdom of Heaven." This was the more significant, that the word "mysteries" had in the growth of ideas and of language come to represent a great religious institution of ancient times.

Among the Ancients, unwonted knowledge was a very dangerous possession; and exalted religious ideas,—such as there were,—preserved themselves from the laugh of the fool and from the curse of the bigot by donning the garb of Obscurity. Philosophers taught one thing to the multitude and quite another to their disciples; and priests catered to the superstitions of the people in public, and in private cherished thoughts they dared scarce lisp to one another. This resulted in systems of outside and inside (exoteric and esoteric) teaching, and careful processes of novitiate and initiation. Great truths were pictured before novices,—as it were in parables,—by curious symbols, solemn processions, impressive rites and dark sayings; and they were misunderstood, except by the keenest trained minds, as it was intended they should be. These systems of philosophic and religious study and of scenic declaration were spoken of in general as "the Mysteries"—of Eleusis—of Isis—of Bacchus: they prevailed very early in Egypt, and later in Cyprus, Syria, Asia Minor and Greece, and probably all over the ancient civilized world.

It is, then, of much interest and meaning that Jesus spoke of the doctrines of the Kingdom of Heaven as "the Mysteries." Indeed, He seems to have appropriated a proverb which was current in the ancient world, and which grew out of the state of things just described. One form of it is found in Plato. "I conceive," quoth Socrates in "Phædo," "that the founders of these mysteries had a real meaning and were not triflers, when they intimated in a figure long ago that he who passed uninitiated and unsanctified into the world below will live in a slough, but that he who arrives there after ini tiation and purification will dwell with the gods; '*for many,*' as they say in the mysteries, '*are the wand-bearers, but few are the mystics!*' meaning, as I interpret the words, the true philosophers." This proverb, or some kindred form of it, Jesus adapted to His uses, changing the words, but keeping the form, in His own oft-repeated utterance: "Many are called, but few are chosen."

Paul, equally impressed by this analogy, declared, "Great is the Mystery of Godliness." To him the Gospel was "the Mystery of Faith," "the Mystery of Christ," "the Mystery of God." It was "the Mystery which hath been hid for ages and from generations, but now is made manifest to His saints. To whom God would make known what is the riches of the glory of this Mystery, which is Christ in you the hope of glory." It was "the Mystery which from the beginning of the world hath been hid in God." The Apostles were "stewards of the Mysteries of God." Paul even described his illumination in preparation for his life's work in these words: "By revelation He made known unto me the Mystery!" His very preaching bore the impress of this great fact as he wrote the Corinthians. "But we speak the wisdom of God in a mystery, even the hidden wisdom; which God ordained before the world to our glory. Which none of the princes of this world knew, for had they known it they would not have crucified the Lord of Glory. But as it is written, 'Eye hath not seen nor ear heard, neither have entered into the heart of man, the things which God hath prepared for them which love Him.'" (Notice that this was spoken by Isaiah, and referred to the at that time future Messianic revelation). "But God hath revealed them unto us by His Spirit. For the Spirit searcheth all things, yea, the deep things of God! But the natural man receiveth not the things of the Spirit of God, for they are foolishness unto him, neither can he know them, because they are spiritually discerned!" Paul was a mystic speaking unto mystics. As he plainly said, "We speak wisdom among them that are perfect!" His initiated, however, were simply the spiritually-minded: his outsiders were the carnally-minded. And there was this grand difference between him and a Greek philosopher or an Egyptian priest, and between Christian doctrine and the Mysteries of Eleusis or Isis; that initiation into the Mystery of Godliness was not exclusive, that knowledge in divine things was not proud, that the wisdom of the Cross was far other than that of the princes of this world, and that the wayfaring man, though a fool, need not,—thanks to the aid of the Divine Spirit,—err therein.

A curious comment upon early Christianity, by a heathen, is preserved to us in the writings of Origen, which shows at once how deep-seated was this notion of esoteric knowledge in the ancient world, and which at the same time indicates how naturally men looked upon the teachings of Jesus as of this general character. The critic is Celsus the Pagan, and he is attacking the Christian faith. He urges: "When the criers call men to other Mysteries they proclaim as follows: 'Let him approach whose hands are pure and whose words are wise.' Let us now hear who those are that are called to the Christian mysteries: 'Whosoever is a sinner, whosoever is unwise, whosoever is a fool, and whosoever, in short, is miserable, him will the Kingdom of God receive!'" Celsus was right in his charge, though foolish enough in his inference. It was the glory of the Christian mysteries that the invitation was general, the truths suited to the needs of all and the only qualification a yearning, humble and teachable spirit.

Indeed, so keenly was this analogy perceived and so eagerly emphasized by the early Christians that, in places, religious instruction literally assumed this form. For centuries in Rome there existed a system of communicating divine things through novitiate and initiation, called Disciplina Arcani, quite like the ancient methods of Eleusinian and Orphic mystery.

It is often complained that the Christian Faith is so full of difficult conceptions and great shadowy truths, that theologians can never agree on any exact statements; and that creeds seem to be the mere garments of current thought, sure, in time, to wear out and to be cast off as rubbish. Historical Theology is accused of unreality, inconsistency and changefulness. And the charge is perfectly true, and necessarily so. It is inevitable, that attempts to grapple the colossal thoughts of Christ and of the Unseen World shall prove often relatively feeble and unsuccessful. It shows only that there are many wand-bearers and few mystics, many called and few chosen. Nothing can be more simple than to expect to find theology—the science of divine things—as exact and comprehensible as a landscape in a looking-glass. It is the demand of a child who, between his tops and his marbles, asks his father to tell him what electricity is, and how the telegraph wires carry thought. Religion is practical and simple; but theology is the most difficult of all sciences,—nay, as a mere science (without spiritual insight) it is impossible. What, after all, is theology but the reverent gaze of a childish but learning faith upon things almost unspeakable. The German poet Richter once said, " If there were no longer anything inexplicable, I should no longer wish to live, neither here nor hereafter."

Take the central Christian Mystery, the God-man, the living, life-giving miracle of human history, Himself the Word made flesh, Immanuel. What a sublime conception, and yet with what background of the mysterious. It is a snow-white pinnacle of divine thought, but rising out of dense clouds, its base all hidden. That God loves the world, despite the mocking testimony of pain and death; that He breathed divinity into a man and made him the Word of God, to utter to men the divine thoughts, purposes and will, and to exhibit in sublime parable of character and mission the Infinite Mercy, and so to win men to virtue and to life eternal, and to become Example, Saviour and Intercessor for all who would heed; what grander conception has ever entered the human mind? And from the stand-point of Spirituality, what can be more inherently probable? If it be not true, then Nature is a more meaningless blank and life itself a more melancholy mystery than any subordinate problem that puzzles the scientist or the philosopher!

But attempt to analyze this central Mystery, and how soon our thinking is found on the Outermost Rim of our mental capacity. How could it be? A God-man, scientifically considered, is a monstrosity of conception; possible, but outside the range of investigation, experience and classification. In ecclesiastical history there is no more melancholy reading than the story of the long and bitter controversies among the Eastern Churches, during several centuries, over the person and nature of Christ. Science here is out of place. Accept or reject, but do not dissect. The doctrine is either a sublime fable or it is a supernatural fact, as high above the play of science as the stars above the mountains.

Or, take the Christian doctrine of the Trinity. What light have theological controversies ever thrown upon it? It is shrouded in all the mystery of Godhood. Jesus barely touches upon the facts; but does not even so much as hint at their philosophy. God is our Father and His Father. God is, God is in Christ, God breathes heavenly influences upon us through His Spirit; and the Father, the Son and the Spirit, these Three are One. What may be involved in this distinction, how radical it is, what bearing it has upon Time and upon human History, and just what lies back of the pictorial words, "Father," "Son" and "Holy Ghost," no one knows, nor at present has any means of determining. The word "person" which occurs in our creeds is used in an extraordinary sense. The term is strained to bear its new and crushing load, as we have no knowledge whatever of any creature with more than one personality. The word covers a mystery. Christianity affirms as vigorously as did Judaism, that "the Lord our God is one Lord"; and no thoughtful Trinitarian at this day would consent to any statement of the doctrine that for one moment put in jeopardy the clear and emphatic enunciation of the divine Unity. As regards the mystery, one must be content to conclude with Daniel Webster, that "we must not expect to understand the arithmetic of heaven."

The doctrine of the Atonement, no less, has its background of impenetrable shadows. The efforts of church fathers and theologians to define in exact words its involved sublimities, simply have served to emphasize the mystery. All philosophies of the Cross have signally failed. And this, notwithstanding the fact that practically the Cross has ever been the mightiest source of power in the personality of Jesus. Its moral influences over human feeling and action have been incalculable. Take, for instance, its sway over the imagination of a man like Paul. The proudest utterance of that great Apostle was this: "I bear in my body the marks of the Lord Jesus." He saw in the voluntary submission and humiliation, suffering and sacrifice of the God-man, bound up therein, the Christly self-denial and heroism of all lands and of all ages. Himself bore crucifixion marks. He could preach only Christ and Him crucified; but this meant, in his broad mind, the utterance of all truth, and the urging of everything that could stimulate the human mind to right thinking, the human heart to unselfish feeling, or the human will to deeds of heroism. He could glory only in the Cross; but lo! this meant a generous enthusiasm in all that ennobled his kind. To Paul the Cross of Christ was a phrase for Virtue suffering in humanity's name; and Christ was the personification and His life the realization of this divine law. But why Virtue must suffer for humanity's sake; why one must endure pain that others may become happy, Paul never explained, presumably because he could not.

In the eighth chapter of this treatise, attention was called to the great law of sacrifice in nature and in history. We saw that vicarious suffering was parabled in the facts of the physical world, that the very brutes acted an unconscious heroism and that every page of the story of mankind had been illuminated with splendid deeds of self-denying prowess or endurance.

All friendship, patriotism, generosity and humanity involved vicarious sacrifice; and indeed it was the universal law of humane life. The mother suffered for her child, the soldier for his country and the martyr for his faith. We saw that no religion could escape the notion of vicarious sacrifice, and that every form of worship, it mattered not when or where, had included in its ceremonial some kind of offering or appeasement, at cost of the devotee. We found this fact mysterious and in a sense irrational and from any natural stand-point inexplicable.

But Revelation justifies it. The Gospel tells us that sacrifice is inherent in Deity and is a law of the divine nature. To deny self,—to give,—is godlike. Well said the Lord Jesus, speaking ultimate verity, "It is better to give than to receive." The history of Jesus was a divine life given to the world, His death was a divine life offered up for the world. It was mysterious, as is all heroism : it was seemingly irrational, as is every form of sacrifice. When the Pharisees mocked the dying prophet on the Cross, the irony of Providence forced them in their intended sarcasm to utter sublimest truth, which at once condemned themselves and exalted their victim: "He saved others: Himself He can not save."

The Atonement of Christ was doubtless foreshadowed by every deed of self-sacrifice that the world had ever known; and since Calvary it has been made reasonable by the daily unselfishness of virtue.

But the philosophical necessity of the Atonement is involved in mystery; and its explanations have been but unsuccessful attempts of the learning, ingenuity and piety of this or that age.

To declare that Jesus placated a wrath in Deity is to picture God as a being of malignity. To insist that He suffered the exact infinite punishment deserved by the elect is to claim a moral impossibility. To say that He showed God's abhorrence for sin, fails to appear in view of the fact that the innocent suffered and the guilty were forgiven. That He vindicated the majesty of law, and so sustained moral government, is undeniable; but how?

It is probable, that of all philosophies of the Atonement, among intelligent orthodox believers, what is called the moral theory is at present most popular. But equally with the others it fails. Christ, it is urged, suffered for moral effect. But does the mother deny herself for the moral effect upon her child? Does the soldier, on the battle-field, posture in death for the eyes of his countrymen? Is the martyr in the flames a self-conscious tragedian? The mother, the patriot, the martyr,—though the moral effect may be and is great and beneficial, —are suffering to *save* the child, the country, the faith. The moral effect of the death of Christ was, as we have seen, immense, and His Cross has become the most vivid and useful of His parables; but He died, if we are to believe His words, to save the world from Sin and Hell. He is at the summit of the law of sacrifice, and the eternal necessities we may not now know.

The dogma of the "New-birth" involves impenetrable mysteries, as Jesus himself plainly declared: "The wind bloweth where it listeth, and thou hearest the sound thereof, but canst not tell whence it cometh and whither it goeth. So is every one that is born of the Spirit." It is hard for us to realize the great force of this simile; but it was patent to Nicodemus and the ancients. In these times the winds have indeed lost their mystery: they have yielded up their secret to an inquisitive science. Man's telegraph outstrips their speed and foretells their coming. Meteorological bureaus, in many important centers, watch, record and predict. They can no longer hide their "whence" nor deceive us as to their "whither." But to the men of Christ's day, air, like fire, water and earth, was an "element,"—impalpable,—life-giving or destructive,—and forever mysterious; and the winds were a perpetual enigma.

Ages have passed away, and though we have made the winds to give an account of themselves, Conversion and the Life unto God remain a daily marvel and no mean part of the "mystery of godliness." That the Divine Being should exert influence upon a soul directly, yet the while unseen and perhaps unfelt, is astounding, awful, inscrutable. Undeniable as a fact, it is inexplicable in philosophy. Books many have been written on the subject, learned analyses have become innumerable and confessions of faith strive after unembarrassed statement and scientific apportionment of the human and the divine; but the enigma is unsolved. "The Breath of Jehovah" is in all its workings as much a mystery to-day as the winds to Nicodemus.

And Resurrection, Immortality, Judgment,

Punishment and Glory are all stupendous truths, but in perfect keeping with the other mysteries of existence. They drop rather than lift a veil of Isis, on which are inscriptions, comforting, but hard to fathom; and he who can discuss them glibly and without reverence is worthy only to be excluded from the Temple of the Unseen and Eternal.

The future abodes of good and of bad are designated in Scripture only by picture-words, as Abraham's Bosom, Paradise, My Father's House, New Jerusalem, or Sheol, Hades, Gehenna, and as Glory, Wrath and Torment; while only picture-words, such as palms and harps, golden bowls and white robes, praises and curses, hint at the future estate and occupation. Revelation on Last Things is the merest glimpse of light, and gives us absolutely no basis for any scientific conclusions as to the place, condition, employments or methods of the future existence. One is only permitted, by faith, to sing—

> "I shall lose this life, it will disappear,
>   With its wonderful mystery:
> Some day it will move no longer here,
>   But will vanish silently.
> But I know I shall find it again once more,
>   In a beauty no song hath told,
> It will meet with me at the Golden Door,
>   And round me forever fold!"

The difficulty of the dogmas of Christianity is not that they involve contradiction or absurdity; but that, while practically of unspeakable meaning to the heart, theoretically they defy analysis. To use an image of Paul's, they are reflected on the dull tarnished bronze mirrors of our human stupidity, and they seem, in consequence, shadowy and unreal.

CONCLUSION.

And now our work is done; and we leave to the candid judgment of the reader our meditations upon the ever-expanding limits of knowledge.

If our treatise has been followed carefully, it must have abundantly appeared; that there is an Outermost Rim for all human thinking, and that there is a Beyond; and that, as the Horizon widens, increasing knowledge lends new majesty to the Unseen and Eternal World.

We have perceived that dogmatism, even in the realm of physical nature and of necessary law, is entirely out of place, and that rather the attitude of every earnest scientist can only be one of reverence, expectancy and teachableness. We have seen how education and progress push back, on every side, the barriers of ignorance; and we have discerned some reason even for believing that the mind of man itself ever expands with the using. While over all the beautiful mysterious World, and over all the events of History, has appeared the inevitable dark shadow of human woe.

This preliminary study, revealing great needs and stirring great yearnings, incited us to hearken attentively for Voices from Beyond.

We sought for meanings in Physical Nature, and discovered, at first glance, in all things and events, a Thoughtfulness other than our own. We found, moreover, an unbroken Succession of causes and effects. We perceived an inveterate and irrefragable Persistency of Law. While in the majestic Movement of things we clearly discerned a Progress of Thought. It was therefore necessary to conclude: that the Physical Universe is one and simple, and that the Thinker of Nature is One and Simple, an Ultimate Intelligence.

Thereupon we turned to the Moral nature of mankind, and it at once appeared that men, by constitution, have a sense of right and wrong, and form clear moral judgments, and that when they come to act upon these judgments they find themselves, within limits, free to choose. It further appeared, that the notions of guilt or innocence attach, necessarily, not only to men's doings and feelings, but to themselves as well; and that moral conduct, good or bad, leaves indelible impress upon character and exercises incalculable influence over destiny. Finally, we saw that the moral consciousness works without any necessary relation to civil courts of justice or to personal thought of reward or punishment. And our conclusion here unavoidably was; that Conscience is as ultimate and absolute as Science or Art, and that, as such, it can be viewed only as the hint of a Moral Government and a Moral Governor, a Judge of all the earth, supreme over all justices and all courts.

Proceeding now to the investigation of the religious nature of mankind, we disclosed the secret of the logical compulsion which had forced us to the conclusions of the two preceding chapters. For we found enthroned in reason an intuitive knowledge of an Absolute Being.

We discovered, also, worship everywhere and universal prayer. A belief in immortality was seen to be a mighty yearning of lofty natures and a natural and logical inference in religious meditation. There resulted a firm conviction that religion is a mental necessity, and worship of some kind an inevitable phenomenon.

Glancing now out upon the varied drama of human history, a new class of facts presented themselves. Certain very interesting laws— of Retributive Justice, of Sacrifice and of Sorrow—appeared inexplicable on any naturalistic or atheistic hypothesis. Rendering history tragic, heroic and pathetic, these great principles seemed designed to subserve the purposes of some lofty religion of integrity, of devotion and of patient faith.

These many Voices from Beyond encouraged us to attack the central mystery of human thought and existence—the Mystery of Godliness.

A brief glance at Hebrew prophecy convinced us that human insight into divine things has, at times, arisen to the level of supernatural and authoritative illumination.

Thereupon we concentrated attention upon Jesus of Nazareth as the superlative religious genius of history; and we mused upon the unexpectedness and entire originality of His character, work and words, confounding to all naturalistic explanations and reductions.

We pondered the vastness of the transformation wrought upon human destiny by the religious development He began and shaped, involving immense social improvement, political revolution, enlargement of ethical outlook and elevation of moral and religious standards.

We studied Christ's method of appeal to spirituality by parables of word, deed and event; and we saw that, in some respects, Christian instruction likened itself to the ancient mysteries.

We challenged the authority of Jesus with the result of an enforced acquiescence in His own great claims, acknowledging Him clearly as a Voice Divine from Beyond.

Finally, we reviewed, in brief, the doctrines of grace as particular mysteries of the Mystery of Godliness, finding that Christian dogmas are parables and hints, suggestive and not exhaustive of truth.

Thus everywhere we have come upon an Outermost Rim; and everywhere have we seen reason to infer a Beyond, unknown but knowable.

And, now, we ask the gentle reader,—not to acquiesce in every opinion expressed, nor to refrain from challenging any seemingly doubtful statement of fact or truth; but simply, in all meditation upon ultimate things, to yield to the sway of the lesson of our grand theme, in the spirit of reverence and in the power of a rational but simple-hearted faith.

Of all periods of Christian history, this wonderful age in which we live most needs the urging of this theme and of its lesson.

The times are not worse than they have been, —they are far better; but every age has its own weaknesses, and our weakness is overweening confidence and failing faith. Christianity is working away from the evils of former centuries, from hierarchy, priestcraft, superstition, intolerance and the like follies; but new conditions have brought new dangers.

Unbelief is widespread and is becoming increasingly prevalent. Infidelity to-day is urged, not as formerly, by outlawed and ill-balanced minds, but by men of learning, character and high standing, who have the ear of the public. Their bold or covert attacks upon religious institutions have not been without deplorable effect.

The evil is the greater that the churches still hold some untenable positions theologically, which they fear to defend and dare not abandon. The yielding, one by one, of these fatal outposts, inspires fear and dismay in the citadel itself.

Moreover, and still worse, inside the churches lurks a scarcely defined and often unconscious but very vigorous skepticism. This is repressed and concealed; but it is on that account the more dangerous. The indications of this are not merely frequent lapses of faith, but, much more, decline of zeal, irregularity in attendance upon public worship, abandonment of private devotion, a discontent with life and all its belongings, an unchristian dread of death, a cynicism that readily believes evil of any person or movement and finally a failure to realize comfort from God's promises. It was said of the people of the Island of Rhodes that they built houses as though they were immortal, but feasted as if they expected to die on the morrow. There are a great many saints who profess to believe in Immortality, and in their libraries, churches and alms-giving indicate a lively hope of everlasting life; who yet, in their inner thoughts and feelings, are less spiritual and more hopeless than barbarians. Their creed is faultless and they have a name to live; but their religion is become a mere formula, a routine, perhaps a heartless and thoughtless parade, wherein is neither salvation for a lost world nor even personal safety from utter downfall of faith and character.

The causes of this state of things we need not analyze. It is pertinent to our object, here, simply to express a conviction that the tap-root of the matter is in the discovery by men in general of the fact involved in the theme of this treatise. Men are perceiving that the old barriers of knowledge and belief are moving outward; and they fail to discern,—what this treatise humbly attempts to show,—the real grandeur and beneficence of this steady expansion of devout thought. They have found that the Outermost Rim is not a hard and fast line of horizon, and they tremble lest in the new prospect Beyond they shall see terrible things, —not realizing that this, the seeming peril of faith, is its necessary condition of largest exercise.

The evil is therefore not without its hopeful elements; and no greater mistake could be made than to suppose that genuine religion or sound theology are in permanent danger. Simply, an unusual strain is put upon earnestness, reverence and faith. Only such as have built upon the sand need fear submersion from this tidal wave of infidelity rolling in from the east: it will try men's souls, it will test foundations—not only of the Christian religion, but of all faith in the unseen, and many doubtless will be submerged and swept away; but ere long it will subside. Nothing good and true can disappear. No single trustful and earnest nature need be dislodged.

It is the part of the wise man not to grow discouraged, but rather to study attentively the problem of present unbelief; that, its causes and conditions discerned, the remedy may be applied and the pestilence stayed. The future is full of promise.

Wisely said Lord Bacon: "The old age of time is the youth of the world." Yea, as the ages roll away, the world shall grow young. Enthusiasm, courage and faith, the virtues of youth, shall characterize the future far more than they have marked the past. Knowledge has endless vistas opening before it. Religion goes forth, conquering and to conquer. Let men fearlessly ascend and observe. The summit of knowledge pierces the heaven of heavens. The horizon they behold is but the Outermost Rim; and an Infinity of Truth and all blessedness of ever-expanding and glorified Life is Beyond.

www.ingramcontent.com/pod-product-compliance
Lightning Source LLC
Chambersburg PA
CBHW020826230426
43666CB00007B/1119